Åsa Katarina Odbäck

Dad's Playbook

How to Become the Dad You Wish You Had

FeelGoodPress.com
Designed by Émile Nelson

Cover Artwork by Åsa Katarina Odbäck, Design by Émile Nelson

Copyright © 2017 Åsa Odbäck & Émile Nelson

First Published in the United States of America by FeelGood Press, 2017

All rights reserved. No part of this work may be reproduced or transmitted in any form by any means, electronic or mechanical, including photocopying and recording, or by any information storage or retrieval system, except as may be expressly permitted by the 1976 Copyright Act or in writing by the publisher.

ISBN 978-0-9984459-3-9

"What an inspirational guide for all parents and parents-to-be. I was very impressed."

Jack Canfield, #1 NYT Bestselling Author, *Chicken Soup for the Soul*

"Parenthood is as demanding a sport as football, hockey or baseball, but all too often mothers and fathers come inte the game entirely unprepared for the task of 'coaching' a brand new human from infancy to adulthood. What the parents need is a good coach. Such an animal can be found in book form in Åsa Odbäck's 'Dad's Playbook' ... This book is easy to read and puts a sport spin on parenting experiences and dilemmas."
Working Parent Magazine

"Dad's Playbook provides parents with instant inspiration to become a better parent through developing new strategies for playing and having more fun with their child... This unique combination of sports and parenthood makes Dad's Playbook a fun way to learn how to play a win-win game for the parent and for the child."
Reviewer's Bookwatch

"The paper and this reviewer got many favorable comments from the community regarding Ms. Odbäck's book..."
Patty Pawlak, Book Reviewer, Hendersonville Star News

"Odbäck uses the world of sports to inspire parents to learn how one can have more fun and at the same time help their children. Included are commonsense pep talks and strategies for a variety of sports."
Santa Barbara News-Press

When I was writing this book I sent out a dollar to some sports stars with a letter saying, "A penny for a thought and a dollar for a sentence to help parents be better parents." One day I opened the mail and there was this dollar, with Tommy Lasorda's very wise comment on it...

"Parents should be role models for their children."

Dedicated To:

**Per, Johannes & Émile
And all other children around the world...**
(Without them, none of us would be parents)

If your parents didn't have any children, there is a good chance that you won't have any.

Clarence Day, Author

Table of Contents

Warm Up!	3
Ready! Set! Go!	5
Prepare to Win!	11
Expect to Win!	37
Pursue Your Potential as a Star Player!	51
Build Your Dream Team!	67
What's Your Game Plan?	79
The Game	89
Coaching	101
Communication	109
Goals	119
Challenging Plays	127
When You Are Losing	137
Winning and Losing	149
Playing the Higher Leagues	157

You build a successful life a day at a time.

Lou Holtz, Football Coach, Notre Dame

Preface

Are you having a happy parenthood?

Your child is very important — and so are you! There are many books about raising children, but how about raising parents? A happy parenthood is important for everyone — *Dad's Playbook* wants to make sure you have yours.

Many parents don't think they have time to read books! That's why *Dad's Playbook* is written so you can grab it and open to any page to get some instant inspiration — even when you just have time for a quick glance.

As a parent you can make an incredible difference in the world — for one child or for many, if you choose to. *Dad's Playbook* wants to support you in making that choice.

We hope this book is going to make a difference in how you view yourself, your child and parenthood because becoming a happy and loving parent is certainly one of the most important things anyone can do.

Boys, baseball is a game where you gotta have fun. You do that winning.

Dave Bristol, Manager, Atlanta Braves

Warm Up!

When they start the game, they don't yell, 'Work Ball.' They say, 'Play ball.'
- Willie Stargell, First Baseman, Pittsburgh Pirates

We learn sports from the day we start to play catch with our parents. When it comes to playing the game of parenthood, on the other hand, there are no camps, personal trainers or coaches to rely on — and "P.E." in school doesn't stand for Parenting Education...

Your Pocket Coach for Parenthood bridges the coaching gap, combining experience, wit and wisdom from the world of sports to assist you with practical coaching on becoming a Champion Parent.

Turn to *Your Pocket Coach* for inspiration on how to improve your game, new strategies for playing with your child, or a pep talk when you are in a slump. And remember, you already have what it takes to lead your family team to the top of the league!

So prepare to play, win — and love it all! You've got an important game to play....

Winning is the name of the game. The more we win, the less you get fired.
- Armand "Bep" Giudolin, Coach, Boston Bruins

If the human body recognized agony and frustration, people would never run marathons, have babies, or play baseball.

Carlton Fisk, Catcher, Chicago White Sox

Ready! Set! Go!

I'd rather hit home runs. You don't have to run as hard.
– Dave Klingman, Outfielder, Chicago Cubs

We are taught that it takes hard work to become successful. But don't we all know hard working people who are not successful at all? It takes *smart* work to be successful.

It takes more energy to resist, procrastinate, worry, or feel guilty than to actually do something. Struggling is hard work — and never fun.

Successful people have clear objectives as to what they want to accomplish, and they know how to break their goals down into small doable steps. Then, when they reach their goals, it often looks so easy, as if they just got lucky. The truth is, they are lucky — to know how to be successful. You can be lucky like that, too!

Bob Gibson is the luckiest pitcher I ever saw. He always pitches the day the other team doesn't score any runs.
– Tim McCarver, Catcher, St. Louis Cardinals

Get Set for Success!

I'm a firm believer that people only do their best at things they truly enjoy. It's difficult to excel at something you don't enjoy.
– Jack Nicklaus, Golf Pro, who at age 46 still enjoyed the game enough to achieve his most amazing tournament win, coming from eighth place on the final day to win the 1986 Masters.

The more you allow yourself to play and have fun as a star player on your family's team, the better you will be as a parent. Your child doesn't want you to work hard at being a perfect parent. Your child wants the two of you to play and have a good time together.

You are already a star to your child. No matter how deep a slump you are in, you are still the star in your child's eyes and heart. And no one can replace you.

You don't have to pitch a perfect game every time for your team to win. Actually, "perfect" is never required. Heart, caring, joy and commitment — these are the marks of a good player in the game of parenthood. Since you are reading this book, you must already be a pretty good player — a winner — because a sure sign of a winner is someone who keeps searching for ways to improve his game. No matter what!

Champions keep playing until they get it right.
– Billie Jean King, Tennis Pro. Life Magazine named King and only 3 other athletes (Babe Ruth, Jackie Robinson and Muhammad Ali) as among the 100 Most Important Americans of the 20th Century.

Remember the first time you held your child in your arms, how a feeling of awe and wonderment spread through your whole being. And as you looked into those trusting eyes you suddenly felt that you were part of something bigger than yourself, able to tap into unlimited resources and greatness and do things you never thought you could for another human being. You were ready to lay down your life to protect your child!

Then and there you promised to coach your child through all the rough spots in life, massage the sore spots with gentle hands and cheer for her no matter what.

> **Once a man has made a commitment to a way of life, he puts the greatest strength in the world behind him. It's something we call heart power. Once a man has made this commitment, nothing will stop him short of success.**
> – Vince Lombardi, Head Coach, Green Bay Packers

When you start to lose sight of what is important in your life, keep those first moments with your child alive inside to remind you that she is a gift for you to take care of for only a short time. Use that time wisely and play the very best you know how.

Love is the name of the game and winning the trust and closeness of your child is more rewarding than any other game there is to play.

Go for It!

Experience is a hard teacher because she gives the test first, the lesson afterward.
– Vernon Law, pitcher, Pittsburgh Pirates

Most of us optimistically sign up for parenthood, then suddenly find ourselves in the Olympics of parenthood — realizing we aren't prepared at all.

When we sign up at a new gym, we don't stand around complaining that the weights are too heavy, the machines are too fast and the treadmill takes too much of our time. We enthusiastically get on with our workout!

As a parent we have the same opportunity to develop greater flexibility and strength, and to become a more successful player. Our children provide us with wonderful opportunities to develop the natural winner in us, not only as parents but in every other game in life — if we are willing to go for it.

When it comes to raising a child, too many of us start to get the hang of the game at the very moment our child is ready to stop playing. And we all know we would do it a lot better if we could just get a second chance to play the great parent we meant to be…

The trouble with baseball is by the time you learn how to play it, you can't play it anymore.
– Frank Howard, Home Run Champion, Washington Senators 154

If you were told you had only a few more months to live, or if you were saved from near death by some miracle, how would you live your life after that? You might take a second look at your life and start to make changes at once.

On Saturday, I ran across a piece of prose from a guy who said, 'Yesterday is history, tomorrow is a mystery, today is a gift. That's why it's called the present.' It just knocked my socks off.
– Larry Riley, Director of Player Personnel, Vancouver Grizzlies

Larry Riley was standing at the gate getting ready to board a commuter flight when he suddenly changed his mind. Riley usually didn't let weather or delays stop him from trying to make it to a game. But this time something told him to go home. So he went to the counter and told them to rewrite his ticket. The commuter plane that Riley was originally booked on crashed outside Detroit, killing everyone on board. From that moment on, Riley's life was changed.

I swing big, with everything I've got. I hit big or I miss big. I like to live as big as I can.
– Babe Ruth, the "Sultan of Swat", N.Y. Yankees

Everyone has the will to win but few have the will to prepare to win.
– Bobby Knight, Basketball Coach, University of Indiana. As a collegian, Knight won ten letters in three different sports.

It is not always the strongest man who wins the fight or the fastest man who wins the race, or the best team that wins the game. In most cases it is the one who wants it the most, the one who has gone out and prepared, who has paid the price.

Tommy Lasorda, Manager, L.A. Dodgers

My attitude has always been... if it's worth playing, it's worth paying the price to win.
– Paul "Bear" Bryant, Football Coach, University of Alabama. In 1981 "Bear" Bryant became the winningest coach in college football history, breaking Amos Alonzo Stagg's record of 314 victories.

Prepare to Win!

Losing vs. Winning Strategies

What strategy? If you're behind in the last two minutes, you foul. If you're ahead, you hold on to the ball. That's all there is to it.
– Doug Moe, Coach, Denver Nuggets

What is your strategy for winning the game of parenthood?

* Where do you choose to look first — at your failures or your accomplishments?
* Do you picture yourself as a loser or a winner when it comes to being a parent ?
* What strategy do you practice most, a losing strategy or a winning one?

Described on the left hand pages in this chapter are common losing strategies, on the right hand pages are the winning ones because...

Winning is a habit. Unfortunately, so is losing.
– Vince Lombardi, Head Coach, Green Bay Packers

Is this Your Losing Strategy?

I used to get angry at myself for every mistake I made... I still get angry at myself for mistakes, but I've learned to shake them off. You don't want to forget your mistakes. You want to learn from them... You've got to put your mistakes into a corner of your mind during games and go on applying yourself to the next play and the rest of the game.
– Jerry West, All-Star Guard, L.A. Lakers

You practice losing by replaying old losing games, mistakes, and misses in your mind. If you keep your mind cluttered with pictures, expectations or thoughts from yesterday — or even yesteryear — you limit your ability to achieve what you want today.

We made too many wrong mistakes.
– Yogi Berra, Hall of Fame Catcher, N.Y. Yankees

We learn by repetition. If you replay the fumbles, wrongs, losses and failures in your life over and over again in your mind, guess what you are practicing.

Practice Winning!
Every Day Is a New Game!

Every day is a new opportunity. You can build on yesterday's success or put its failures behind and start over again. That's the way life is. With a new game every day.
– Bob Feller, Pitcher, Cleveland Indians

You practice winning by learning from yesterday's mistakes and using them to your advantage, rather than dwelling on or regretting them. Focus instead on your successes and make them the stepping stones to reaching your next level as a Champion. Replay your favorite games in your mind often. And remind yourself of your successes, of the good times, the joy and the improvements you have made.

Remember, there is no such thing as a perfect parent — heart, caring, understanding, and commitment are the marks of a good player in the game of parenthood. No matter how good you think other parents are, keep in mind that everyone needs practice to be a star player.

There'll be two busses leaving the hotel for the park tomorrow. The 2 o'clock bus will be for those of you who need a little extra work. The empty bus will leave at 5 o'clock.
– Dave Bristol, Manger, S.F. Giants

The Losing Strategy Of Comfort

We're a lot more comfortable breathing the air we can see.
– Mychal Thomspon, Center, Lakers, on why the team plays so well in Los Angeles.

Most of us prefer to keep doing the same thing we are used to — even if we don't like it, know it's not good for us, or realize it won't take us where we'd like to go. We still prefer the comfort of what's familiar to the discomfort and fear of change.

Then our children come along and nothing stays the same. The more we resist the change, the more painful the growing pains become. Children inevitably take us far beyond our comfort zones.

We have an interior 'comfort zone' that we want to be in. Picture a good club golfer playing Jack Nicklaus. His self-image is probably that he is a good golfer, but is not good enough to beat Nicklaus. If he beat Nicklaus, he would be uncomfortable with the demands of his new self-image. So he does whatever he can to get back in that comfort zone, even if it means missing a two-foot putt on the 18th green.
- Dennis Conner, U.S. Olympic Sailor

The Winning Strategy Of Change

Failure is not fatal, but failure to change might be.
– John Wooden, Basketball Coach, UCLA

When you embrace the opportunity to grow and learn how to play new games, parenting is like signing up for a first-class gym — it's open twenty-four hours a day.

Your child will provide you with excellent training opportunities on how to not only to be a Champion Parent, but also how to be a winner in the game of life — if you choose to work with the change, rather than against it.

If you'll not settle for anything less than the best, you will be amazed at how much you can do with your lives. You'll be amazed at how much you can rise in the world.
– Vince Lombardi, Coach, Green Bay Packers

The Losing Strategy Of Not Having Time

I learned a long time ago to have [an assistant coach] with three kids. He'll be in his office working at eight every morning so he doesn't have to deal with getting the kids off to school.
– Dick Versace, Coach, Indiana Pacers

Are you one of those parents who would spend more time with your kids if you only had the time? Are you just too busy making a living, working out, taking care of the car, paying the bills, keeping up with the news, etc.?

Next up is Fernando Gonzalez, who is not playing tonight.
– Jerry Coleman, Player, Manager, Announcer, N.Y. Yankees and San Diego Padres

Taking the Time to Win

Now, I know that very often you 'just don't have the time.' In spite of that, if you really want to improve, you will have to make the decision, and then the commitment. There are no shortcuts. You must lay the proper foundation.
– Severino Ballestros, Pro Golfer

Every day you waste is one you can never make up.
– George Allen, Football Coach, Washington Redskins and L.A. Rams

The Losing Strategy Of Having No Energy

Soccer proved to be the toughest and Motocross Racing was second. Pro Football came in eighth. It is presumed that baseball players were not tested because doctors did not want to awaken them.
– John Sonderegger, commenting on a study of the most strenuous sport.

We often excuse ourselves from winning the parental championship with the explanation that we don't have the "energy" left over to become the great parent we would like to be.

If you think of yourself as being stressed out, too tired or too old — rather than young, active, fun and playful — you are feeding yourself defeatist messages. It might be a comfortable habit, but it's not a winning one.

> **Slumps are like a soft bed. They're easy to get into and hard to get out of.**
> – Johnny Bench, Catcher, Cincinnati Reds

The Winning Strategy Of Going for it 100%

You can't get much done in life if you only work on the days you feel good.
– Jerry West, Guard, L.A. Lakers

We have all had the experience of being totally tired out, and then getting 100% involved with something and suddenly having the energy to go on for hours.

After working all day, allow yourself to play. Although it can be hard to shift gears, playing with your child will give you new energy and keep you healthy, young and in good shape.

One aspect of training for success is learning to focus 100% on one thing at a time — and really going for it. When we go for anything fully, it becomes fun. It's a lot easier to do 100% than 99%!

You not only play, but also share both the good and bad times. When the game is over I just want to look at myself in the mirror – win or lose – and know I gave it everything I had, that I didn't let anyone down. That's my number one priority. I want to know that I played the game straight from the heart.
– Joe Montana, Quarterback, S.F. 49ers. With Montana as quarterback, the 49ers won four Super Bowls. In three of them, he was the Most Valuable Player.

The Losing Strategy Of "One Day I Will..."

So many ideas come to you and you want to try them all, but you can't. You are like a mosquito in a nudist camp. You don't know where to start.
– Reggie Jackson, Outfielder, Oakland A's

If you often feel overwhelmed and never get started with things, you already know the strategy that you use to sabotage your games. Feeling overwhelmed!

Feeling overwhelmed is an effective way to justify staying in your comfort zone and never getting to all those things that you think you should do with your child — one day...

Children have been conceived and born during a Mike Hargow at-bat.
– Norm Hitzges, Announcer. His comment on the first baseman's lengthy preparations which earned him the nickname "The Human Rain Delay."

The Winning Strategy Of Starting Today

The first thing a beginner needs to learn is how to pick up the ball.
– Arthur Hoppe, Syndicated Tennis Columnist, in the debate over what the first thing a tennis player need to learn – forehand, backhand, serve or volley.

Instead of focusing on all the things you ought to change, start by doing one little thing differently — nothing big that you can't keep up for more than a few days. Just choose one single little thing in your game that you will work on or do differently in the coming month.

For example, if you often correct and criticize your child, start making it a habit to comment on something he does well every day. Or, if you have stopped touching your child, reach out and hug him every day. Or make sure you spend X amount of time alone with your child each day.

It is amazing how a little change can create big results.

If you don't get on first, you can't score a run.
– Enos Slaughter, Outfielder, St. Louis Cardinals

The Losing Strategy Of Being Distracted

Houston Astros Manager Hal Lanier had all TVs removed from the clubhouse because too many players, instead of taking infield practice, spent most of their time watching "Wheel of Fortune."

You can't be thinking about too many things. Relief pitchers have to get into a zone of their own. I just hope I'm stupid enough.
– Dan Quisenberry, Pitcher, Kansas City Royals

When playing with your child, do you keep your focus on what's really going on — or do you often make mental shopping lists, worry about work, glance at the TV or try to read the newspaper?

You wouldn't think about all those other things while playing a game of tennis that you wanted to win...

The Winning Strategy Of Focus

It's when you look at a cheerleader and don't notice her body.
– Al McGuire, Basketball Coach, Marquette University, talking focus at a pressure game.

Watch the action at a playground or a park. How many parents really focus on playing with their child? How many only watch the child while keeping an eye on their wristwatch or reading the newspaper? Which parents look happy?

Respect your child and be present when you spend time together. Even if it takes an initial effort to get yourself going, don't just push the swing like a robot. Talk to your child, swing with him, or clown around and make it his best swing ever!

Focus is the key. Focus on your child when you're with him — both of you will have more fun. And you deserve to have more fun and joy in your life!

You always have to focus in life on what you want to achieve.
– Michael Jordan, Basketball All-Star, Chicago Bulls

Losing Sight of Your Priorities

There are three things in my life which I really love: God, my family and baseball. The only problem — once baseball season starts, I change the order around a bit.
– Al Gallagher, Third Baseman, S.F. Giants

Do you burn up all your energy in other areas of life and then expect your relationship with your child to simply be there when you have a few minutes left over to play?

If you tell your child you love her and would do anything for her, but can't take the time to be there when she needs you, has a school play, or just wants to talk, are you really living up to your word?

There is nothing in the world I wouldn't do for Walter O'Malley. There's nothing he wouldn't do for me. There's the way it is. We go through life doing nothing for each other.
– Gene Autry, Owner, California Angeles

Prioritize to Win

You prove your worth with your actions, not with your mouth.
– Pat Riley, Coach, L.A. Lakers, N.Y. Knicks and Miami Heat

Remember what comes first in your life — even after the season has started. Make sure you set your priorities rather than let circumstances or others set them for you.

To reach peak performance in any area of life, it's important to set priorities and stick to them. What you make important, you will succeed in.

Maybe you need to prioritize your relationship with your child before a small crisis explodes into a major one. No one would consider it strange if you needed to take extra time to deal with a job crisis. Think twice the next time your child asks you to do something, and try to find a way to say "yes."

Winning makes everyone a star.
– Lenny Wilkens, Guard, Seattle Supersonics. Wilkens was an NBA All Star nine times as a player, and four times as a coach, Wilkens is the most prolific coach of all time and a three-time inductee into the hall of fame.

The Losing Strategy Of Being a Trapped Kid

When I was a little kid, I used to imagine animals running under my bed. I told my dad, and he solved the problem quickly. He cut the legs off the bed.
– Lou Brock, Outfielder, St. Louis Cardinals

Did you have a bad childhood that left a scared child imprisoned inside of you? When scared, sad or hurt, that same child can make a fuss in the middle of a game causing you to act immature and do things you later shake your head over and wonder why you did them.

How old would you be if you didn't know how old you were?
– Satchel Paige, Hall of Fame Pitcher, who was over 40 in his rookie year in the majors with Cleveland, and probably 59 when he pitched for the Kansas City Athletics in 1965 — which makes him the oldest player in major league history.

If you feel out of control, have problems with your feelings or act immature toward your child, you might take a look at one of the many books about dealing with your inner child. Or talk to someone who can help and support you.

The Winning Strategy
Of Working With Yourself

The stupidest thing in the world is a man with his own gifts trying to act like someone else. You can be taught and you can be inspired. But you've still got to be you.
– Willie Mays, Hall of Fame Outfielder, S.F. Giants

There is no such thing as a fully grown up, mature person. We all have a child inside, no matter how old our bodies are. If you can relate to the child inside of you with loving acceptance and support, your inner child will be more willing to help you play and have fun with your child. Your inner child can also give you valuable insights about how it feels to be small and helpless.

Your inner child can be the most precious resource when it comes to raising your child, and you can raise the two of you together if you choose to be sensitive and aware of what is going on inside of you. It's never too late to create a good childhood for yourself!

I don't think we can win every game. Just the next one.
– Lou Holtz, Football Coach, Notre Dame

The Losing Strategy Of Sitting on the Bench

You can't get rich sitting on the bench – but I'm giving it a try.
– Phil Niekro Sr., father of Phil and Joe, pitchers for the Atlanta Braves and Houston Astros

Even though we might have many good reasons for not playing, sitting on the bench could be the most expensive mistake we ever make. We risk missing out on the most important play of in our life — being a parent.

I took the two most expensive aspirins in history.
– Wally Pipp, First Baseman, N.Y. Yankees, who took a day off because of illness and was replaced that day by Lou Gehrig, who continued to replace him for the next 2130 games.

The Winning Strategy Of Getting Up

A champion is one who gets up when he can't see.
– Jack Dempsey, Heavyweight Champion of the world

Dempsey's first title defense in December of 1887 started in a downpour that soon flooded the ring and forced the fight to be moved. The rain turned to snow and the fight went 45 rounds before Dempsey finally won.

In sports the players often get bruised and break bones, yet they keep playing — sometimes not even aware of the injury until the game is over.

Getting 100% involved with your child will help relieve you from your worries and daily stress. Play and laughter are the best healers and relaxants for your body and mind. And unlike a long night of drinking, they have no side effects.

There is no better tonic for an injured hockey player than scoring a goal.
– Bobby Hull, All-Star Hockey Player, Detroit Red Wings, who scored 913 goals in his NHL career

The Losing Strategy Of Fight or Flight

The Mets have shown me ways to lose I never knew existed.
– Casey Stengel, Manager, N.Y. Yankees and N.Y. Mets

Do you feel you're in a slump as a parent? Are you not only losing, but having your whole game fall apart? Is your sweet darling child suddenly playing like he's been traded to the opposing team and wants nothing more than to thwart you? He booms his serves at you as he tries to ace you at every opportunity.

In retaliation, you instinctively go on the defensive. Adrenaline pumps you up, shuts off your normal senses and prepares you for fight – or flight.

I left because of illness and fatigue. The fans were sick and tired of me.
– John Ralston, Coach, Denver Broncos

The Winning Strategy Of Commitment

Some parents leave their team when they are needed the most — when things get challenging. As one setting an example for your child about how to deal with the stresses of life, it would be wise take a look at your own level of commitment — especially when things get tough.

> **Individual commitment to a group effort — that is what makes a team work, a company work, a society work, a civilization work.**
> – Vince Lombardi, Coach, Green Bay Packers, winning coach of the first two Super Bowls

The key to success in every area of life is commitment. To create what you want, you must commit to it 100%. Commit to play the best you know how — no matter what.

> **Nobody who ever gave his best regretted it.**
> – George "Papa Bear" Halas, Coach, Chicago Bears, and one of the founding fathers of the National Football League

The Losing Strategy Of Blaming

A man may make many mistakes, but he isn't a failure until he starts blaming someone else.
– John Wooden, Basketball Coach, UCLA. Wooden led the Bruins to 10 NCAA titles, by far the most of any coach.

Sometimes we blame our work, our spouse, another person, or something else when our strategy isn't working the way we want it to.

Maybe you have to work all the time, so you see very little of your child. Or perhaps you are divorced and live apart from your child. Or you feel that you have to compete with another parent figure in your child's life who seems so much better at it than you are...

The man who complains about the way the ball bounces is likely the one who dropped it.
– Lou Holtz, Football Coach, Notre Dame

The Winning Strategy Of Taking Responsibility

I've always felt it was not up to anyone else to make me give my best.
– Akeem Olajuwon, Center, Houston Rockets

When you say things like, "You make me so angry!" remember that your child or spouse does not have the power to dictate your feelings. Nobody can control you or your emotions — unless you let them.

Others do what they do. You are the one who is in control of you, your games and the way you play.

I don't look for excuses when we lose, and I don't buy excuses when we win.
– Dave Cowens, Center, Boston Celtics

The Losing Strategy Of Getting Discouraged

I knew I was in trouble when the guy was clocking me with a sundial.
– Joe Magrane, Pitcher, St. Louis Cardinals

If you recognize a lot of the losing strategies as your own, don't get discouraged — that's great! Knowing your losing strategy is the first step to success. Most of us don't have any idea what's wrong, so we can't even start to fix it.

If you are ready to acknowledge what you are doing, and that you have other choices, you are well on your way to winning!

The choice is yours — to continue doing the same things as always and getting the same results as always — or to try one of the winning strategies. Check it out!

With the kind of year I had, I'm ready to try anything.
– Paul Householder, Outfielder, Cincinnati Reds, on getting engaged after a season in which he batted .211

Try a New Winning Strategy

You can't change everything at once, but what you can do is pick out one strategy that appeals to you and really give it a try.

Don't forget! You are the first pick, the star player, on your parent-child team, no matter how deep a slump you are in.

———————————————

It took me 12 seconds to become an overnight sensation.
– Toby Harrah, Third Baseman, Cleveland Indians

———————————————————————————

When you and your child are winning together, the sun shines on your game and your efforts are all home runs, touchdowns and slam dunks. Together you are Rookie of the Year, Most Valuable Player and Star of the Dream Team!

That feeling is worth more than any first prize trophy.

So what are you waiting for? It's never too late! Start practicing a new strategy for winning — now!

I'm working on a new pitch. It's called a strike.
– Jim Kern, Pitcher, Cleveland Indians

I expect to win every time I tee up.

Lee Trevin, Professional Golfer

Expect to Win!

Have You Got An Attitude?

I knew we were in trouble when we got there and their cheerleaders were bigger than us.
– Matt McDonagh, 13-year-old soccer player

* Do you expect things to go wrong, people to act badly or yourself to lose?
* Do you often find that things go just as badly as you think they will?
* Do you find satisfaction in saying, "What did I say?!"
* Do you look at your cup as half empty instead of half full?

A part in each of us tries very hard to make sure we do not disappoint ourselves. If we have negative expectations, our unconscious success strategy is to make ourselves right by fulfilling those expectations.

A good night tonight is 0-for-4 and don't get hit in the head.
– Oscar Gamble, Designated Hitter, Cleveland Indians, about batting against Nolan Ryan

Your Attitude About You

My volley is blah. I'm a dead elephant on the court. My serve has no sting and I am confused. Other than that I'm a fine player.
– Mona Schallau, Tennis Pro

As parents, it's easy to feel like we're not doing enough. Many of us *want* to be better parents, but, with all the other things going on, we often end up parenting on autopilot, instead. At the end of the day, many of us go to bed beating ourselves up for not being the best parents we could be, and we start to feel disconnected and isolated because we just can't seem to get it right.

When we constantly tell ourselves that we are not good parents, we start living a self-fulfilling prophecy. We start to lose that close connection with our loved ones, and our own playfulness and enthusiasm fades away because we constantly make ourselves feel bad. Eventually, nothing seems exciting and we just feel stressed out and tired of everything — and, most of all, disappointed in ourselves.

Negative attitudes are a sort of poison.
– Fran Tarkenton, Quarterback, Minnesota Vikings

The big thing is not what happens to us in life, but what we do about what happens to us.
– George Allen, Coach, Washington Redskins

What we do inside of ourselves determines what we do out in the world. Our expectations and attitudes will either limit us or enable us to expand and meet new, challenging goals.

Don't accept your own excuses and feelings of inadequacy as eternal truths. If you have a negative attitude, think you don't have what it takes or feel that you'll always be a loser, no one is going to try to prove you wrong!

If you tell yourself you can't be a great parent, guess what? You can't.

Confidence is a lot of this game or any game. If you don't think you can, you won't.
– Jerry West, "Mr.Clutch", Guard, Coach, General Manager, L.A. Lakers

I'm not going to allow him to pick up our baby until it's at least five years old.

Ed Nealy's Wife, after a game in which the NBA player dropped many passes

Other People's Attitudes About Us

I'd have booed too. I looked up in the stands and I thought I saw my wife and kids booing.
– Jerry Reynolds, Coach, Sacramento Kings, after a Kings' loss to the L.A. Lakers

From the moment we are born we look to others to tell and show us who we are — or more accurately, who they think, fear or hope we are. As children we adopt our parents' opinions about ourselves, and even later, when we rebel against them, we still fear deep inside that they were right.

I will never understand how she can ski down a mountain at 50 or 60 miles an hour, then come home and fall down the stairs.
– Heather Percy, mother of Karen Percy, Bronze Medalist Skier on the Canadian Olympic Team

If we learn that we are impractical, stupid, terrible, hopeless, ugly, and so forth, and continue to live with those negative attitudes about ourselves, we will attract people who will confirm them. We need to actively show ourselves how great we really can be, and that begins with changing our attitudes about ourselves.

A Three-Pointer

If there's something that has to be done to win a game, I've always thought I could do it. Obviously, there have been times when I've failed. But I haven't thought that I was going to fail. I've always thought I could do what was necessary.
– Michael Jordan, Basketball All-Star

I think fans say 'He's big, he can run, he's funny, he dives on the floor, he dunks with his left or right hand, and he's got lots of tricks in his bag.' If I was a fan, I'd come watch me play, too.
– Shaquille O'Neal, Center, L.A. Lakers

I'll always remember this as the night that Michael Jordan and I combined to score 70 points.
– Stacey King, Center, Chicago Bulls, after scoring one point on a day Jordan scored 69

A New Attitude

Errors are part of my image. One night in Pittsburgh, thirty thousand fans gave me a standing ovation when I caught a hot dog wrapper on the fly.
– Dick Stuart, First Baseman, Pittsburgh Pirates

Changing your attitude about yourself is the number one thing you can do to make a major change in your life.

Before you go to sleep, congratulate yourself on all the things you did well during the day, like letting someone in before you on the highway, making your child laugh, or bringing in enough money to feed your family. If you are in a relationship, you can make it a habit to express your appreciation of your partner, too.

If you had a hard day at work, instead of beating yourself up by going over your mistakes, pat yourself on the back and thank yourself for making it through the whole day.

Make it a habit to tell yourself good things about yourself in the shower, in the car, waiting in line, when you can't sleep... A part of you will start to look for all of the good things you do, and you will start feeling better about yourself. Pretty soon, a new positive self-image will form inside of you.

If I only had a little humility I would be perfect.
– Ted Turner, Owner, Atlanta Braves and Hawks, Winner of America's Cup

It's a good thing Brian was a third child, or he would have been the only one.

Kathy Bosworth, mother of Brian Bosworth, Linebacker, Seattle Seahawks

Your Attitude About Your Child

He (Dad) said my weakness would stand out like a neon sign. If I couldn't dribble with my left hand or if I had the habit of being lazy on the defense, everybody would know it. He told me that in basketball I couldn't hide.
– Magic Johnson, 3-time NBA MVP

You can't hide anything from your children — like lie detectors they can sense whatever we're trying to hide!

If your child is giving you a hard time, take an honest look at your attitude about your child. It's natural to be irritated by your kids sometimes, or feel jealousy, envy or resentment. But sometimes we are ashamed to admit we have negative emotions about our own children — as if that makes us bad parents — so we feel guilty and repress them.

Feelings sometimes need to be expressed for us to be able to let go of them. So, when you're feeling guilty about negative thoughts you may have along these lines, find someone you can talk to. Or write down your feelings and burn the piece of paper afterwards. Just make sure that you take responsibility — don't dump the negative feelings on your child.

If you are holding negative feelings about your child inside, it affects the relationship between the two of you, and your child might start to act out your repressed feelings in a way that could drive anyone nuts.

If Mother Teresa played in the NBA, after one encounter with Laimbeer, she'd want to fight.
– Jan Hubbard, Newsday Sportswriter

He's one of the smartest guys to put on sneakers since Einstein.

Stan Morrison, Basketball Coach, USC, talking about John Sundvold

A Winning Attitude about Your Child

He not only can play the piano. He can pick it up.
– Mrs. John Shehelessy, talking about Mike Reid, a 6-foot-3, 255-pound Defensive Tackle for the Cincinnati Bengals, who played the piano for her music club.

A supportive and winning attitude about your child is essential if you want to encourage her to be a winner. Instead of dwelling on things that might bother you about your child, make a list of all the wonderful things about her — who she is, what she does, how she does things, and especially try to appreciate things about your child that might be foreign to you. Read that list often.

You never know who you are raising! At this moment our future stars and presidents are being raised by regular parents, like you. Or maybe you are raising someone unique, someone who will help you see and experience things differently and take you beyond your limitations.

Make sure you are open to see how your child is special — all children are — but all children do not have parents who support individuality. Don't try to make your child a copy of you, or what you would have liked to be; instead, appreciate your child for who she is, and she will become the very best there is.

He's quick enough to play tennis by himself.
– Jim Killingsworth, Basketball Coach, Texas Christian University, speaking about Paul Pressey of Tulsa

Your Attitude about Parenthood

The challenges you have with your kid are often blessings in disguise. Maybe that's hard to see sometimes, but try look for the learning, for how you can grow and improve from each challenge.

> A popular deaf-mute boxer, Danny London, took an explosive punch to the head that caused him to lose the fight, but he couldn't believe his luck when he shook his head and discovered he could once again hear and speak.

When you learn to master the lessons your child brings to you as a parent, the victory will be even sweeter. And you will also be able to apply your increased skills to other areas of your life — and become a true winner.

Losers have tons of variety. Champions take pride in just learning to hit the same old boring winners.
– Vic Braden, Tennis Instructor

You've got to love what you're doing. If you love it, you can overcome any handicap or the soreness of all the aches and pains, and continue to play for a long, long time.
– Gordie Howe, Hall of Fame Hockey Player. Howe played 25 seasons with the Detroit Red Wings, 20 of them after suffering a serious head injury.

Remember that love is the intent of the parenting game. Whether it is giving, receiving, understanding, experiencing, learning or testing, the purpose of every game you play with your child is still loving. Your success will be proportional to how much you desire to create more loving and joy for your team.

As in any game, a close relationship with your child will test all of your good and bad qualities. The good news is that when you are able to handle the tests, you will find that this close and loving relationship with your child is one of the most rewarding experiences you can have.

Look for positive things in the relationship with your child, dwell on your good times, laugh and celebrate your child every opportunity you get! If you feel great about the two of you, it will not only affect your relationship in a positive way but it also will affect your child's sense of self-worth.

We lost 14 straight. Then we had a game rained out and it felt so good we threw a victory dinner.
– Vernon "Lefty" Gomez, about his short experience as a minor league manager.

Great effort springs naturally from a great attitude.

Pat Riley, Head Coach, L.A. Lakers, N.Y. Knicks and Miami Heat. In his first seven seasons coaching the Lakers, Pat Riley led the team to the NBA finals five times, winning the title four of those times.

Pursue Your Potential As a Star Player!

Make the Effort!

Working hard becomes a habit, a serious kind of fun. You get self satisfaction from pushing yourself to the limit, knowing that all the effort is going to pay off.
– Mary Lou Retton, Gold Medal-Winning US Olympic Gymnast, Associated Press' Woman Athlete of the Year in 1984

Equipped with your new winning strategy and positive attitudes, you are now ready to pursue your potential as a star player. It's not just going to happen, it takes practice and work. There will be challenges to overcome, like in any game we play. It's not easy to get a small puck into the net behind a goalie, either. Still, people can do it... on ice skates!

And there's only one way to build that kind of confidence. That is to practice often enough and long enough. Deep down inside, you've got to know that you're capable.
– Jimmy Connors, Tennis Champion. Connors began practicing tennis at the age of three and went on to rank number one in the world for five years in a row, from 1974 through 1978.

The first thing is to know your faults and then take on a systematic plan of correcting them. You know the saying about a chain being only as strong as its weakest link. The same can be said of the chain of skill a man forges.

Babe Ruth, Outfielder, N.Y. Yankees

Keep Your Eye on the Ball!

I din't see him do anything. After all, I've only got two pairs of eyes.
– Nestor Chylak, American League Umpire, after being criticized in the playoffs following a violent argument.

In parenthood, as in any game, the ability to observe what is really going on is crucial. When we train ourselves to take a look at what we are doing, and acknowledge our own strategies to get what we want, we reach a deeper understanding of the games we play — and the games others play.

By learning to neutrally observe these games we play, we take a big leap along the path to victory — even if it doesn't look too flattering at first sight. First we need to acknowledge what is going on, accept it, and then look at how to improve it.

Coaches have to watch for what they don't want to see and listen to what they don't want to hear.
– John Madden, Football Coach, Oakland Raiders

The nice thing about Cedeno is that he can play all three outfield positions — at the same time.
– Gene Mauch, Manager, Montreal Expos, talking about Caeser Cedeno, Outfielder, Houston Astros

No parent can be everything to his child. Still, we try! Have you ever seen a father busily working to build a model for his child, while the child sits there staring off into the distance, bored out of his mind. In his eagerness to make this perfect train set or model airplane, the father is missing the goal of creating a fun, shared experience.

I don't get a big charge out of being the leading scorer… I just try to do what has to be done for us to win. That might be anything at any time — defense, rebounding, passing. I get satisfaction out of being a team player.
– Kareem Abdul-Jabbar, six-time NBA Most Valuable Player

What Kind of Player Are You?

I'm not a Mercedes. I'm a Volkswagen. They get a lot of mileage out of me, but I'm not pretty.
– Dan Quisenberry, Relief Pitcher, Kansas City Royals

Start with taking a good look at yourself. What kind of player are you? Maybe you're a goalie. Check whether you are wearing a lot of protection. Is your padding preventing you from being flexible? Are you always standing alone, defending something? Or perhaps are you a front row expert, commentator, or a referee…?

We often choose to play the same role over and over again, each time expecting a different result. If playing the referee — always handing out penalties — hasn't created the closeness and win-win game you want with your child, try something different this time. Your child is growing and getting better every day. Are you?

In my prime I could have handled Michael Jordan. Of course, he would be only 12 years old.
– Jerry Sloan, Guard, Chicago Bulls

The season starts too early and finishes too late and there are too many games in between.

Bill Veeck, Owner, Chicago White Sox

What Kind of Game Are You Playing?

The clock doesn't matter in baseball. Time stands still or moves backward. Theoretically, one game could go on forever. Some seem to.
– Herb Caen, Columnist, San Francisco Chronicle

Baseball is a game that takes time out of existence. In theory, a baseball game could go on forever if a team never makes the third out. Is that how you feel about being a parent at times?

Even as a parent, you need a break once in a while. If you are taking care of your child alone, don't try to play the super hero. If you can't afford to pay someone to help you, try setting up a support system with relatives, friends, or other parents to help each other out. To play well you need some time for yourself, even if it's just a couple of hours over the weekend when you exchange kids with another parent.

If there are two of you taking care of the child, then take turns providing breaks. And don't forget the importance of creating quality time alone for the two of you. Couples need a foundation of closeness that is independent of being parents. Happy parents are a wonderful gift to a child!

Take care of yourself first, so you can take care of your child.

It's the quality of the time you spend practicing that counts, not the length of time.
– Jimmy Connors, Tennis Champion, who retired in 1993 as the all-time leader on the Men's tour with 109 tournament victories.

I think he is some kind of alien. I think he was kidnapped and brought back here, some kind of ET thing.

Donnie Walsh, speaking of Michael Jordan whose moves on a basketball court sometimes seemed to defy gravity.

What Kind of Player is Your Child?

John Boozer used to go into the clubhouse and spit on the ceiling. When it dropped back down he could catch it in his mouth. He was a breed all of his own. He would try to turn guys' stomachs. He had no scruples. He was a beaut, and a real nice guy.
– Clay Dalrymple, Catcher, Philadelphia Phillies, describing pitcher John Boozer

They say that beauty is in the eye of the beholder. Every gym and health club has mirrors for us to exercise in front of, to help us improve and correct our workouts. People around us also act like mirrors, especially people close to us.

If what you see irritates you, remember that the person you are looking at is acting as a mirror. What are they mirroring back to you that you don't like about yourself?

We don't slump, chew with an open mouth, or scream in front of mirror. Instead we usually straighten our backs, hold in our stomachs and put on big smiles. Try to show your best side in the same way to your most observant mirror image, your child. Your child imitates everything you do from the first minute of her life — your posture, gestures, way of speaking, your attitudes...

The best thing wrong with Jack Fisher, is nothing.
– Casey Stengal, Hall of Fame Baseball Manager, N.Y. Yankees and N.Y. Mets

If you are going to be a champion, you must be willing to pay a greater price than your opponent will ever pay.

Charles "Bud" Wilkinson, Football Coach, University of Oklahoma, whose team won a record 47 games in a row from 1953 to 1957.

Your Opponent...
Who Are You Playing?

Fear is your best friend or your worst enemy. It's like fire. If you can control it, it can cook for you; it can heat your house. If you can't control it, it will burn everything around you and destroy you.

– Cus D'Amato, Boxing Manager. D'Amato guided Floyd Patterson to the Heavyweight Title, and Jose Torres to the Lightweight Title, and later discovered Mike Tyson.

Who is your opponent? Who is playing on the opposite team and preventing you from being the winner you deserve to be? Your spouse? Your child? Your boss, childhood, finances...?

The reason we often become losers instead of winners is that we look outside for that opponent to our success, when he is often hidden inside ourselves.

Our fears are what prevent us from being winners in the games we play in life: fear of success, fear of failure, fear of change, fear of being disappointed, fear of rejection, fear of losing, and fear of being unworthy — or fear of taking an honest look at the games we play...

You look at a player being brave. He's afraid, or he wouldn't be brave. If he isn't afraid, he's stupid.

– Joe Torre, All-Star Catcher, then Manager, N.Y. Mets, Atlanta Braves and St. Louis Cardinals

Accepting Our Fears

You never really cancel the fear of losing; you keep challenging it.

– Arthur Ashe, Tennis Pro. Ashe was the first black male to win a national title – the first U.S. Open in 1968 and the Wimbledon singles title in 1975.

A fear we all share is the fear of losing, whether it's someone we love, something that's important to us, a game…

When our children express one of our own fears, we immediately react as if someone bumped into a big bruise. Our first instinct might be to try to force the child to push away her fear, as we have done.

Instead of accepting fear as a part of life, we deny it and push it deeper into our unconscious where it controls us, out of reach of our conscious will.

You can't hit what you can't see.

– Walter "Big Train" Johnson, Hall of Fame Pitcher, Washington Senators. Johnson's nickname came from sportswriter Grantland Rice, and reflected the speed of his fastball. In 1927, despite Babe Ruth's 60 home runs for the Yankees, Johnson pitched the rival Senators to the American League pennant.

Provide your child with a safe space to express his fears to you and don't deny him the right to be afraid. Saying things like, "It's nothing to be afraid of!" or "Don't act like a baby!" only puts guilt and shame on top of the fear that the child has to deal with.

Help your child by validating his feelings and putting the fear into perspective. "It's okay to be scared, I can see how this seems scary to you," or "Let's take a look at this together and you can tell me how you feel." Let your child know that you were afraid of things, too, at his age. Reassure your child with loving support so that, instead of feeding his fear, you are building his confidence and strength.

Everyone has some fear. A man who has no fear belongs in a mental institution. Or on special teams.
– Walt Michaels, Head Coach, N.Y. Jets

It's important to admit to ourselves and let our children know that we all have pain, loss and failure inside of us, and that the fear of getting hurt is a part of most games in life. It is up to us to either let it block us or strengthen us to go on.

If your name wasn't on the list, you were cut. Mine wasn't on the list. I looked and looked for my name– but it wasn't there. I went through that day numb. I sat through my classes. I had to wait until after school to go home. That's when I hurried to my house and closed the door to my room and I cried so hard. It was all I wanted – to play on that team.
– Michael Jordan, the only player to win the NBA Most Valuable Player award and the Defensive Player of the Year award in the same season, in 1986.

Fear of Losing

To win you have to risk loss.
– Jean-Claude Killy, winner of three gold medals in skiing in the 1968 Winter Olympics.

We take the power out of fear by laughing, playing, loving and having fun.

Fear arises from the refusal to pay the price of sacrificing the drama, despair and hopelessness of being a loser. So if you have the courage to start to play more, laugh more and love more, you are well on your way to becoming a winner and a champion.

To take the power out of the fear of losing, play games with your child where the point is to make as many mistakes as possible. Have fun with it. Everyone performs much better when relaxed and having fun. No matter what the results are, you and your child are winners when you're learning to laugh and play together.

We never force our kids to climb any further than they feel comfortable with, if that's 30 feet, 10, or whatever, that's perfectly fine. The kid is here for his climb. If the father keeps saying, 'Go higher, go higher!' we offer the father a harness. 'Please, you do it first!' We are not here to conquer the tree or our fears, we are here to be with the tree and ourselves, and have fun.
– Peter Jenkins, Founder of Tree Climbers International

Don't be frightened if things seem difficult in the beginning. That's only the initial impression. The important thing is not to retreat; you have to master yourself. This ability to conquer oneself is no doubt the most precious of all the things the sport bestows on us.
– Olga Korbut, Gymnast. Picked as an alternate on the Soviet gymnastics team in the 1972 Munich Olympics, Korbut won three gold medals and one silver, changed the style of womens' gymnastics and was selected as the Associated Press Female Athlete of the Year.

We need to remind ourselves that our opponent — our fear — is never bigger or stronger than we are. Fear is only a part of us. We have a lot of of other resources inside of ourselves that can help us overcome fear if we just acknowledge what we are afraid of.

By learning to acknowledge and deal with our own fears, we teach our children to do the same. As a parent, you are the number one role model, and your child learns more by watching how you handle situations in your life than she does from anything else.

You are really never playing an opponent. You are playing yourself, your own highest standard, and when you reach your limits, that is real joy.
– Arthur Ashe, Tennis Champion. Ashe retired from tennis following a heart attack in 1980 and then became a champion of human rights. After contracting AIDS from a blood transfusion in 1983, Ashe established and supported the Arthur Ashe foundation to help defeat AIDS.

The way a team plays as a whole determines its success. You may have the greatest bunch of individual stars in the world, but if they don't play together, the club won't be worth a dime.

Babe Ruth, Pitcher and Outfielder, Boston Red Sox, N.Y. Yankees and Boston Braves

Build Your Dream Team!

The secret of winning football games is working more as a team, less as individuals. I play not my eleven best, but my best eleven.
– Knute Rockne, Football Coach, Notre Dame, whose team, with the famous Four Horsemen backfield, went undefeated in 1924, 1929, and 1930.

With your new success strategies, positive attitude and willingness to pull in the effort it takes, you are now ready to build your dream team.

You can take the best team and the worst team and line them up and you would find very little physical difference. You would find an emotional difference. The winning team has dedication... They will not accept defeat.
– Merlin Olsen, All-American Tackle. Olsen was a mainstay of one of the best professional defensive lines of the 1960s, the L.A. Rams' "Fearsome Foursome."

Playing in Hell or For The Angels?

The Angels are the first team I've ever been on where I feel I belong. They are all nuts, too.
– Jimmy Piersall, Outfielder, L.A. Angels. Piersall was known for his crazy antics on the field, such as running the bases backwards and sliding into home plate following a home run.

What is your challenge as a team? Are you a short-distance sprinter with a child who runs marathons? Or is your child a mountain climber, but you are afraid of heights? If your child is an ice skater with good form and grace and you are a goalie with a mouthpiece and stick, you might have to make some adjustments before the two of you can create your Dream Team.

Find areas where you match — where you both can enjoy participating in the same game, but be open to learning new things, as well. Find out what really works for you and your teammate, and how you can improve so as to have more fun.

Passing the ball is what I like best, because if I can get the ball to a guy and he scores and I see the gleam in his eye when he's running back down the court, it's the greatest feeling in the world.
– Larry Bird, Forward, Boston Celtics. In addition to being a top scorer, Bird was perhaps the greatest passing forward ever, with 5695 assists in his NBA career.

A baseball team can't win with just pitchers. Don't limit your child by allowing her to express only one side of her personality or by invariably doing the same things together.

> **It gets so you actually forget your own hurt at times, so strong is the desire to help your club – the men you work and play with every day – come out on top.**
> – Mickey Mantle, Outfielder, N.Y. Yankees. Throughout his career with the Yankees, Mantle was troubled by osteomyelitis and problems with his knee, By age 30, he had to have both his legs heavily taped before every game. Still, in his 18 years with the Yankees, Mantle's team won the pennant 12 times.

Your team needs more than one kind of player to win. By allowing for different expressions and methods of play, you give your child a chance to experience many different aspects of herself and you, thus building a foundation of friendship that will last longer than any game. You might also be surprised at what you discover about yourself by playing a different game or using a new technique.

It means I'm going to be an example to my teammates of what having a winning attitude is all about... It means I'll challenge myself, I'll set goals. It means I'll think 'we' and not 'me' every time I step onto the court.

Magic Johnson, who retired from the NBA as the career record holder in assists.

Assisting – The Magic Touch

Fred Brophy, Montreal Westmounts, was known for being the most aggressive goalie in hockey and the only goalie to skate all the way to the opposite side of the ice and score a goal... twice!

When playing with your child, you need to be careful that you don't become a player who does everything. Instead, assist your child in doing things for himself and finding his own solutions.

The result-oriented approach of focusing on what needs to be done and then fixing it yourself doesn't always work so well on the parent-child team. At times, a more successful game plan is to assist your teammate in solving problems his own way. Focus your approach on cheering and encouraging your teammate. Create opportunities for your child to score and make your child the star on your team!

Erwin "Magic" Johnson, Jr was one of the best ever at creating opportunities for his teammates to score. It is said that Magic was the only player that could take just three shots and still dominate a game. Among his many achievements is his being named Most Valuable Player in 1987, 1989 and 1990. He was also the Most Valuable Player of the Gold Medal winning Dream Team at the 1992 Olympics.

Be a Consistent Player

They throw, I swing. Every once in a while they're throwing where I'm swinging and I get a hit.
– "Lefty" Gomez, Pitcher, N.Y. Yankees, explaining his slugging strategy. Lefty was always poking fun at his own hitting. Sometimes when he called for a bat, the bat boy would ask "What are you planning to do with it?"

Is that how your child feels about you — worried about what you are going to do next? Your teammates need to feel secure in order for them to play well.

If you're on top of the world one day and let your child do anything she wants, then you're down and intolerant toward her the next — you're helping to create confusion and insecurity in your child. Now she will have to test you during every game to know what the limits are. She may also blame herself if you get angry or are unhappy, and both of you will end up feeling like losers.

A pro plays whether he wants to or not.
– Carl Yaztremski, Outfielder, Boston Red Sox. "Yaz" won the triple crown in 1967 with a 3.26 batting average, 44 home runs and 112 RBIs. His career lasted 23 seasons, 1961-1983

If you are usually upbeat and enthusiastic and then find yourself having a bad day and acting cross, let your child know it has nothing to do with him. Explain what's going on and why you are upset or troubled. To be open and honest with a child and ask for his support is an unfamiliar approach for many parents.

> **It isn't hard to be good from time to time in sport. What's tough is being good every day.**
> – Willie Mays, Outfielder, N.Y. And S.F. Giants. Mays had a career .302 batting average, with 3,283 hits, including 660 home runs and 1,903 RBIs.

Try it! Tell your child you will play as well as you can, but you need his support in the game so you don't blow it. And then sacrifice your pain or worries and focus on winning with your child.

> **Winning is not a sometimes thing; it's an all-time thing.**
> – Vince Lombardi, Coach, Green Bay Packers and Washington Redskins. Lombardi's teams won 105 of their 146 games.

I love exercise. I could watch it all day.
– Bill Russell, Center, Boston Celtics

Instead of sitting around the television, start to exercise with your kids. In addition to sports, you can fly a kite, bike, run, go to the park, put on some music and dance, jump rope or take a walk in the forest and hug the trees — just get moving!

All that running and exercise can do for you is make you healthy.
– Denny McLain, Pitcher, Detroit Tigers and Washington Senators. In 1968, McLain became the first and only 30-game winner in the majors since Dizzy Dean.

Creative Play

The Fosbury Flop is a "heads first, face up" method used by most high jumpers today. When Dick Fosbury introduced it to the world at the 1968 Olympic Games in Mexico City, everyone thought he was collapsing as he jumped in this new weird fashion — and won the Gold Medal!

Doing something new and different can seem strange or even threatening to some people. However, if what we have done so far hasn't given us the level of success we want, we need to be open to try something new. Be creative and go for new plays in pursuing your dream.

If you usually watch TV together with your child at night, try some variety: draw together, play charades, sing crazy songs, go bowling, sign up for an acting class together, bake a cake or cook a new dish. Better yet, let your kids teach you something new.

Kids love new things. Newness is the key to excitement. Do something old in a new way with your child, like eating a picnic on the floor instead of having dinner at the table, sleeping out under the stars instead of in your beds…

He was the only player I ever saw who had the whole arena standing every time he rushed down the ice. You see, when Shore carried the puck, you were always sure something would happen.
– Hammy Moore, Trainer, Boston Bruins, talking about Eddie Shore, four-time Most Valuable Player in the NHL

Practice Fun!

You can't practice being miserable.
– Bum Philips, Coach, Houston Oilers, speaking about not being prepared for the below zero temperature in Cleveland.

But you can practice having fun, and exercise humor and laughter as much as possible. Take the seriousness out of your game and make it okay for your children to fight you in a fun way, joke around and play with you.

Blow ping pong balls and try to catch them
Make faces at each other in front of a mirror
Have an argument without any understandable words. Argue your point!
Have an old-fashioned pillow fight.

If they were faked, you would see me in more of them.
– Rod Gilbert, Hockey Player, N.Y. Rangers, when asked if hockey fights are faked.

Baseball is supposed to be a non-contact sport, but our hitters seem to be taking that literally.
– Larry Doughty, General Manager, Pittsburgh Pirates

Touch, hug, dance, and wrestle with your child — a good physical workout handles lots of tension and emotion in a fun way for both of you! Fight for fun when you are close and happy; it will also take the seriousness out of your next fight. We all learn much better when we're relaxed and having fun. Remember, play ball not work ball.

Roll around in bed or on the floor – play-wrestle.
Have a water balloon fight – preferably outside!
* *Go to a park and throw leaves at each other, or snowballs if it's winter.*
Blow soap bubbles at each other, but wear sunglasses to protect your eyes.
Throw cotton balls at each other – it's very hard to hit!

Fans never fall asleep at our games because they're afraid they might get hit with a pass.
– George Raveling, Basketball Coach, Washington State

My best game plan is to sit on the bench and call out specific instructions like, 'C'mon Boog,'' 'Get hold of one Frank,'' or 'Let's go Brooks.'

Earl Weaver, Manager, Baltimore Orioles. In 17 seasons as a manager, Weaver won 90 or more games 10 times.

What's Your Game Plan?

Go and Get Them Or Get Them Going?

The most important measure of how good a game I'd played was how much better I'd made my teammates play.
– Bill Russell, Center, Boston Celtics. Russell holds the record for most NBA championships with an astounding 11 titles in his 13 seasons.

You need to bring out the best in your child, and support, motivate and inspire her to play the very best she knows how.

Whatever your goal in life, be proud of every day that you are able to work in that direction.
– Chris Evert, Tennis Pro. Evert's father was a tennis pro before she became one. His highest ranking had been 11th, while his daughter won 18 singles grand slam tournaments and three doubles titles.

If your work is not fired with enthusiasm, you will be fired with enthusiasm.

John Mazur, Head Coach, New England Patriots

Team Spirit

Enthusiasm is everything. It must be as taut and vibrating as a guitar string.
– Pele, Soccer Star who led Brazil to three World Cup championships

To win in our lives we need to get in contact with our childhood level enthusiasm — the enthusiasm to learn, discover and achieve new things. It is said that the word "enthusiasm" means energy from God. Whatever you do that makes you enthusiastic, tap into that source.

Find out what makes you and your teammates enthusiastic and how you can get the energy of enthusiasm flowing to carry your team to victory.

Success is not the result of spontaneous combustion. You must set yourself on fire.
– Fred Shero, Coach, Philadelphia Flyers

Giving Support

I hit .450 when I was batting clean-up for my high school team. Of course, my mother was the official scorer.
– Jack Billingham, Pitcher, Cincinnati Reds. In a major league career of 13 seasons, without his mother as scorekeeper, Billingham batted .111

Let your child know that you are on his side no matter what. When playing with your child, practice gentleness, patience and loving — and give 150% of your support.

Assist your child through every game. Like a catcher supporting his pitcher, let your loving support for your child create a battery that can provide the energy for any tough play he has to work through.

Hold a positive image of your child, express it often in every way you can think of, and let him feel that you appreciate, adore, respect and admire him. He's your Babe...

If he hits a home run, he's gonna get the cheers, and if he strikes out, he's still gonna get the cheers.
– Wes Ferrel, Pitcher, N.Y. Yankees, speaking about Babe Ruth

Every team needs huggers. These are the guys you sign so you can hug 'em after you've won instead of having to hug the guys who play and sweat.
– Tommy Varden, Assistant Coach, Centenary, talking about back-up players

Hockey players always skate by their goalie and pat him with their sticks before the game. Touch is essential in creating a safe and supportive atmosphere for your child. It fosters team spirit and helps you get in touch with your own heart.

When a child is small, most parents feel safe hugging, kissing and holding him. But the older the child gets, the more careful many parents become about touching. Studies have shown how important touch is for a child's development and well-being. Your child needs your caring touch.

Sometimes a child expresses this need for physical contact with you by tackling you or bumping into you. Be creative – grab him for a hug or carry him around like an airplane!

The key to beating the Dodgers is to keep them from hugging each other too much.
– Greg Nettles, Third Baseman, N.Y. Yankees

Keeping Agreements

If you say you're going to do it, and you go out and do it, it ain't bragging.

- Dizzy Dean, Hall of Fame Pitcher, St. Louis Cardinals. When his brother Paul joined the Cardinals in 1934, Dean promised a pennant and that "me and Paul will win between 45 and 50 games this year." They went out and did it, too — Paul won 19 games and Dizzy 30, leading St. Louis to the pennant.

If you say you are going to do something, keep your word — do it! A part of us monitors whether we do what we say we will, and this part plays a huge role in developing our self-esteem and self-respect. If we continually let others down, we also let ourselves down.

Your child's trust is a precious part of your play. Don't forfeit that trust by making commitments you can't keep.

It doesn't take talent to be on time.
-Peter Reiser, Coach, California Angels

Playing Honestly

Most pitchers fear losing their fastball and, since I don't have one, the only thing I have to fear is fear itself.
-Dan Quisenberry, Pitcher, Kansas City Royals

By being honest with your child, you never need to fear falling off your pedestal or losing face because your relationship is build on a solid foundation of honesty and support.

Share how you handle your challenges with your child. This gives her a chance to learn how to deal with similar situations later on. Don't dump your problems on her, or misuse her trust and support. Simply share from your heart what's going on without dwelling on it.

Kids are extremely caring beings. If you're honest with them and share your thought and feelings, you might be surprised at the amazing responses you'll get.

Success is a peace of mind in knowing that you did your best to become the best that you are capable of becoming.
-John Wooden, Basketball Coach, UCLA, and one of only four people to be inducted to the Basketball Hall of Fame as both player and coach.

Desire

Desire is the most important factor in the success of any athlete.
– Willie Shoemaker, Jockey. Shoemaker was born prematurely and not expected to live. Having fought his way into the world, and despite his size and weight, he was undefeated as a high school wrestler and a successful Golden Gloves boxer. Even after he suffered a broken neck and was paralyzed in an auto accident at age 59, it only took 6 months for Shoemaker to return to training horses.

"Desire! That's the one secret of every man's career. Not education. Not being born with hidden talents. Desire."
– Bobby Unser, Race Car Driver

You're not going to get far until you have a burning desire to excel.
– Nolan Ryan, Pitcher, Houston Astros. In the 1986 National League Championship series, Ryan shut down the N.Y. Mets while pitching on a broken ankle.

Commitment

I've never known anybody to achieve anything without overcoming adversity.
– Lou Holtz, Football Coach, University of Arkansas

No matter what you have to overcome, don't let anything stand in the way of your dream. We always possess something stronger than the obstacles placed in our path – and that something is the power within to overcome them.

The grand star of the 1986 New York City Marathon was a man who took more than 98 hours to complete it. His name was Bob Wieland, a Vietnam veteran. He had no legs. He used his arms to pull himself over the 26-mile, 383-yard route.

You have to be a dedicated person. You have to want to do it more than anything else. You have to want to be number one.
– Mario Andretti, Race Car Driver

Baseball was designed for American television – 15 seconds of action and 3-minute breaks for commercials.

Dogdan Chruscicki, Radio Announcer

The Game

Breaks, Rules and Foul Play

He only eats one meal a day. Unfortunately, it lasts all day.
– Mack McCarthy, Assistant Coach, talking about Charles Barkley, the "Round Mound of Rebound," when he was at Auburn University

All games include breaks. So do what players do — take short breaks every now and again. Breathe, relax, drink something... whatever, but take care of yourself and your child.

Some parents push their child around for hours while shopping, without taking a break in a park or having a snack. Then they get angry with their child when he refuses to play the game their way or begins to fuss and demand things to get attention.

If your child starts to whine or act cranky, it's time for a break — you're probably into overtime! You have made your star player go too long. Now you need to make sure you don't have a burnout. Supply your team with what they need to play well.

He thinks a balanced meal is a Big Mac in each hand.
– Pat Williams, General Manager, Orlando Magic

Anticipation and Preparation

Before leaving a place, prepare your child and explain that it will soon be time to leave. If you suddenly say, "Okay, now we have to leave," your child will often protest. Instead, ask him if there's anything he needs to do before leaving. By doing that, you give your child time to adjust and make him feel like a part of the decision to go.

If you want to raise your child to be a winner, get him used to feeling like one. Don't push him into situations where he will come out looking like a loser.

> **It's a long year and there are a lot of highs and lows. Sometimes it's difficult to get ready to play, but if they are not ready, they know it. If you can cause them to be ready, and be prepared for all situations they'll have to face, they'll be motivated.**
> – Tom Landry, Football Coach, Dallas Cowboys

If you are going on a trip, the name of the game is preparation! You need to plan your time on the road or in the air thoroughly. Bring along some activities to keep your child occupied and add a few of his favorite snacks. Traveling with a tired and hungry child isn't fun for anyone! Also, you might consider buying small presents that your child can open if you're going on a long excursion. This is a small cost to pay for an easy, successful journey.

Failure to prepare is preparing to fail.
– John Wooden, Basketball Coach, UCLA

Protections

It was the most difficult year I've had since puberty.
– Dave Bliss, Coach, SMU

Kids don't wear protection like grown-ups do. We get hurt and put on a layer of protection to make sure it doesn't happen again. After another hurt, we add another layer and another, until we shut most things out.

Children are wide open and unprotected from hurt. It's our job to protect them and teach them how to protect themselves when they need to, and also to show them it's safe to be open and vulnerable sometimes.

Many of us wear protection all the time. Then, when we try to be open and intimate, all that protection we wear gets in the way. As you encourage your child to be open with you, it's important to practice being open, yourself.

Remember that the intensity of strong light, loud noises and hectic energy affects your child. Don't shock her system into closing down. Her sensitive openness is a gift for you and your team. Honor, cherish and learn from it.

It's called a nudist ball; it's got nothing on it.
– Phil Hennigan, Pitcher, Cleveland Indiands, talking about his new pitch

Controlling the Game

I had no chance of controlling a ball game until I first controlled myself.
– Carl Hubbell, Pitcher, New York Giants

Trying to control anyone but yourself is a losing game. You can't really do it, but we still try. If there's something you want from someone, be flexible and don't push your perspective too far. If you force somebody to do something, it might feel like you scored for a short time, but it won't count if you're offside.

You slowly build a fence between you and your child when you act controlling and unreasonable as a parent. This is something you may later regret, especially when you find it difficult to get close to your child. A teenager who has been controlled by his parents for many years will most likely rebel against them as soon as he feels some power to take charge of his own life. At that time, it may be too late to start working as a team.

A leader is interested in finding the best way – not in having his own way.
– John Wooden, Basketball Coach, UCLA

Quiet Calm

Concentrating on his "Dazzling Footwork," the boxer Harvey Gatley exhausted himself and fell without a punch. He was counted out after 47 seconds in the first round.

Pay attention to your child and try not to get too preoccupied with your own dazzling footwork that might cause you to fall. Sometimes we stress through life by doing, doing, doing and we don't allow ourselves to take a deep breath and just be. Children need the time to take a breath and just be, too — they need time for daydreaming, thinking, feeling and finding out things about themselves and their world.

Some parents are so eager to give their children a head start in the game that they transport them around to different activities almost every hour of the day. It's great to stimulate your child and provide support for participating in different activities, but remember to keep a balance in your child's life. It's not only about doing and achieving, it's also about reflecting and being. Take time to quiet down and watch a sunset together, smell the flowers, or curl up in front of the fire and just be. Help your child keep the essence of innocence, curiosity and peace that she was born with.

Baseball was made for kids, and grown-ups only screw it up.

– Wes Westrum, Hall of Fame Pitcher

The fewer rules a coach has, the fewer there are for a player to break.

John Madden, Coach, Oakland Raiders

Rules of the Game

I won't say the umpiring is bad in our leagues, but we'd be better off playing on the honor system.
– Dick Williams, Manager, Oakland A's

Rules are usually based on a *no*. Most of us, at whatever age, seem to have one thing in common — when we run up against a *no*, we like to test it, put the brakes on or try to get around it.

Always check if there is a reasonable request behind your child's wish to do something before you push the automatic *no* button. If your child wants something that is not in her best interest, present an alternative that might work better. By only saying *no* at times when there really is no other option, you show your child that when you say *no* it's for a very good reason.

Before you make a rule, be sure it is absolutely necessary and that you are willing to enforce it. Look for ways you can say *yes*, too. In being reasonable, fair and caring, you help your child develop their own inner guidance and a sense of responsibility.

If you always tell the truth, you don't have anything to remember.
– Dick Motta, Coach, Chicago Bulls, and the first coach of the Dallas Mavericks

The Good Bad Boys!

You just have to play for yourself. For your own pride and self-respect.
– Dick Butkus, Linebacker, Chicago Bears

Often we say *no* or *you can't* to our children because we don't want to spoil them. But, just ask yourself, if you want something that's fairly reasonable, does it make you a better person if you don't get it?

Children and grown-ups are not spoiled by feeling worthy of having what they want. Many young lives are spoiled by their parents who were raised to believe they don't deserve anything, and then go on to deny their children in the same way. Not feeling worthy of getting what we want is a major obstacle to success.

Because of us there's the no-clothesline rule, the no-spearing rule, the no-hitting-out-of-bounds rule, the no-fumbling-forward-in-the-last-two-minutes-of-the-game rule, the no-throwing-helmets rule, and the no-Stickum rule. So you see, we're not all bad.
– Ted Hendricks, Linebacker, Oakland Raiders, claiming that the "bad boys" of football have a good side to them.

If you still think of your child as unworthy of having a good education, or as irresponsible and in need of a lot of restrictions, it doesn't matter how good a school you put your child into. Unconsciously he is going to prove you right. The flip side of this is that if you treat him as a wise and important individual who can be trusted, he will also prove you right.

The role of my parents was perfect. They were helpful but never interfered with my tennis — they gave assistance all the time but never told me what to do, when to practice, when to play tournaments. It's like taking piano lessons when you're young. If they had told me I had to practice four hours a day and pushed it down my throat, I would have quit tennis.
– Björn Borg, Swedish tennis champion

Support your child's growth by allowing her to share in the decisions that concern her as early as she is able to communicate and participate.

Freedom is something we either gradually grow into or suddenly grab for ourselves as it's denied to us.

Be willing to negotiate and cooperate with your child. Communicate to find ways to agree instead of using your authority. Keep the rules down to a minimum, but agree on how to enforce the rules you make. Also, be willing to negotiate some rules for yourself in the interaction with your children, such as being on time or keeping your promises. Decide what the penalty will be if you're late or break your word.

A lot of parents think kids ought to learn responsibility from work, and I've always said 'Baloney.' Kids learn leadership and organization from games, from having fun.
– John Madden, Coach, Oakland Raiders

In 1964 during Nassau Speed Walk, a Grand Prix for Volkswagens, A.J. Foyt and Dan Gurney came up with an outrageous strategy for winning. Gurney, in his high-powered VW, drove up behind Foyt when the 100-mile race started, and began pushing him at high speed, leaving the rest of the field far behind. With just a quarter of a mile to go, Gurney passed and zoomed in 1st followed by Foyt in 2nd. Gurney was immediately disqualified because his specially-built power car didn't meet the regulations of a production VW. Instead, Foyt was declared the winner and collected the prize money! A remarkable feat considering the fact that he was driving the slowest car in the entire race!

Cheating

If your child lies or tries to cheat once in a while, don't dramatize the issue. Deal with it in a matter of fact way and go on. A lot of attention might enforce a certain behavior, so making a big fuss about something might actually be a way you teach your child to do more of it. Most of us have tried to cheat or lie at least one time in our life.

I try not to break the rules, but merely to test their elasticity.
– Bill Veeck, Owner, Chicago White Sox

Instead of penalties, numerous rules and time-outs, let your child know that regardless of whether or not he gets away with cheating, one person will always know — himself.

Our self-esteem and sense of worth determines how we perform in life, and gives us a picture of ourselves that we project to others. When we cheat or lie, we start to lose our self-respect and sense of worth, and begin to look down at ourselves. That prevents us from feeling worthy of getting what we want, even in completely different areas of life. So when we cheat, we might actually cheat ourselves out of winning.

Boys must learn that the one thing that is important is their self-respect. Keep your self-respect and you win. Lose your self-respect and you are defeated, no matter how the world looks at you.
– Red "The Galloping Ghost" Grange, Halfback, University of Illinois and Chicago Bears

The number one factor for happiness and success in life is how you feel about yourself. Be sure to play in a way that makes you feel good about you.

Coach's Corner

Coaching is teaching, and it's taking the time out when a guy doesn't do it right to tell why he doesn't do it right. Show him how to do it right.
– Mike Ditka, Coach, Chicago Bears

Always have a plan and believe in it. I tell my coaches not to compromise. Nothing good happens by accident.
– Chuck Knox, Coach, L.A. Rams

Coaching

Parents should be role models for their children.
– Tommy Lasorda, Hall of Fame Baseball Manager

We all know that a child learns from observing what we do, and not from listening to what we tell them to do. One of the most important jobs we have as parents is to be role models for our children. Being a good role model means showing — not just telling — your child how to make positive choices and handle the challenges in life, through your own behavior, attitudes and strategies.

You don't have to be perfect to set a good example for your child. Nobody is perfect. If they were, no one would be able to stand them. What we can do is watch what we say more carefully and strive to always do the best we know how.

A person always doing his or her best becomes a natural leader, just by example.
– Joe DiMaggio, "The Yankee Clipper," Outfielder, N.Y. Yankees
Dimaggio was a three-time winner of the Most Valuable Player award. Beginning in 1936, when DiMaggio joined the Yankees, the team won four consecutive world championships.

If the coach is organized, everything falls into place. If he has self-discipline, the team has discipline. If he's dedicated, the team is dedicated. Everything revolves around the head coach. He's the one who has to make the team go.
– Ray Nitschke, Linebacker, Green Bay Packers. The coach of the Packers at that time was Vince Lombardi.

Many people think that being a role model for your child means being perfect and not making any mistakes. That's a mistake! If you give your child this false impression, she will be terrified about making mistakes and go to any extreme to avoid taking risks. Then, when she does make a mistake she won't have a clue how to handle it.

The fear of failure and general fear of making mistakes can sometimes make it hard for us to admit when we make a wrong decision. As parents, we feel it might ruin our kids' respect for us. In fact, admitting when we are wrong and apologizing for it is not losing, it's actually an important step toward showing our children how to win, even through mistakes.

By showing your child that mistakes are not bad — that they are actually stepping stones to excellence — you help him to develop a great attitude and the courage to try new things.

He who is not courageous enough to take risks will accomplish nothing in life.
– Muhammad Ali

Be a Role Model!

I made some dumb pitches when I had to.
– Dave La Point, Pitcher, Pittsburgh Pirates

Admit you make mistakes, especially after you have made one with your child. Apologize and get on with it.

Your child is watching and will learn how to handle her mistakes from you. If your child becomes defensive, tries to lie or hide mistakes, or is unwilling to take risks, you don't need to look much further than in the mirror to see why.

By doing your best to admit when you stumble, you inspire your child to "go for the gold" and deal with challenges as they arise.

I try not to take life too seriously. You're not going to get out of it alive anyway.
– Karl Douglas, Quarterback, Baltimore Colts

I'm trying not to put too much pressure on myself, but I think I'm overcompensating. I'm putting too much pressure on myself not to put too much pressure on myself.

Dan Bilardello, Catcher, Pittsburgh Pirates

Go for Reasonable Expectations

If I'd done everything I was supposed to, I'd be leading the league in homers, have the highest batting average, have given $100,000 to the cancer fund and be married to Marie Osmond.
– Clint Hurdle, Rookie, Kansas City Royals. In his major league career that lasted 10 seasons, Hurdle hit 32 home runs and batted .259.

It's great to have goals and objectives, but don't put too much pressure on yourself to get everything right on the first play. It's better to collect a lot of smaller victories than fail to meet your grandiose goal time after time.

Take things gradually and secure each small success before reaching out to do more. Taking on too much, or having unrealistically inflated expectations of yourself or your child can sabotage your game and slow down your success.

This year we plan to run and shoot, next season we hope to run and score.
– Billy Tubbs, Basketball Coach, University of Oklahoma

Expert Advice

He'll scream from the 60th row of the bleachers that you missed a marginal call in the center of the interior line and then won't be able to find his car in the parking lot.
– Jim Tunny, NFL Referee, describing the typical fan

People are always willing to give advice. But, when you're taking advice from someone on how to raise your kids, it's wise to check out their kids.

Each generation does its best to raise children, but sometimes we need to break traditions and discontinue old mistakes, like using violence against our children, misusing our authority or ignoring a child's cry or need to express himself.

What might be considered spoiling a child fifty years ago may be a natural, everyday thing in today's terms. Parents now have access to a lot more information and resources. We need to improve parenthood, as well as everything else. Listen with care to the experts. There are many out there who "know" exactly what they would do in your place.

Ruth made a grave mistake when he gave up pitching. Working once a week, he might have lasted a long time and become a great star.
– Tris Speaker, Manager, Cleveland Indians, in 1921, speaking about Babe Ruth's change from being a great pitcher to becoming one of the single greatest hitters of all time.

There are two theories on hitting the knuckleball. Unfortunately, neither of them works.
– Charlie Lau, Hitting Instructor, Chicago White Sox

If you're getting lost in theories and other people's opinions about how to raise your child, don't forget that experts' opinions about child raising have changed many times and will keep on doing so.

When you feel overwhelmed or uncertain of what to do, remember that you and your child are the true experts when it comes to your team. Listen to what your most valuable player — your child — has to say.

When in doubt, treat your child as you would have liked to be treated as a child, and be the parent you always wished you had when you were growing up.

Heart, caring, understanding, commitment — these are the marks of a good parent. Love your child, over and over again…

It's important to be a self-starter. Nobody is going to wind you up in the morning and give you a pep talk and push you out. You have to have a firm faith and belief in yourself.
– Lou Holtz, Football Coach, Notre Dame

Show, Don't Tell!

William Ellsworth Hoy (1862-1961), a deaf and mute Major League Baseball player, was called "Dummy," but he didn't mind the nickname. In fact, he liked it. It was to help "Dummy" that umpires started to use the hand signals for balls and strikes that are standard today. Over his 14-year career, Hoy had 2,044 hits and a batting average of .287. Instead of applauding Dummy, the fans waved thousands of white handkerchiefs from the stands to show their appreciation for him.

Communication

Signals, Calls and Throwing the Flag

Winners never quit and quitters never win.
– Vince Lombardi, Coach, Green Bay Packers

* Do you care as much for your child as the fans cared about Dummy?
* Are you willing to hang in there and work things out even if you have to develop your own way of communication to understand each other?
*Are you prepared to be creative and go the extra mile for your child?

Many parents think communication just means talking. But, really, the most important part of communicating with your child is listening.

Tests show that most of us listen at only 25% efficiency — 75% of the original message is lost!

To really listen to your child and hear what she has to say, listen not only to the words but to the emotions, body language and what is not being said. We all need to work on listening with an open heart instead of an open mouth.

Listen up because I have nothing to say and I'm just going to say it once.
– Yogi Berra, 18-time All Star Catcher

Safe!

I told him, 'Son, I can't understand it with you. Is it ignorance or apathy?' He said, 'Coach, I don't know and I don't care.'
– Frank Layden, Coach, Utah Jazz

Even though it sometimes doesn't feel like it, there is always a way to communicate. Instead of reacting to a challenging expression, listen to what your child is trying to communicate to you.

Sometimes all your child wants is to be heard. If you want to be on a winning team together, you need to build up a level of trust with your child and make it safe for him to express feelings.

Create a safe place inside of you for your child to express what he needs to. Let go of your own defense mechanism for a moment, even if you feel attacked. Try not to interrupt or correct what he's attempting to say — just listen carefully and meet what is said with understanding rather than punishment. And instead of reacting negatively to your child's expression, relate to the problem at hand and choose a more positive response.

I don't have any problems – just concerns.
– Eddie Stanky, Manager, St. Louis Cardinals

Mets outfielder Cleon Jones asked the umpire if one could get thrown out of a game for thinking. The umpire said "No." Cleon Jones then replied, "Well, then I think you're doing a lousy job."

If your child is having trouble telling you something, try to support her by repeating the points you hear her make — even if you don't agree with them. Repeating them back reassures your child that you hear what she's saying. Then check to see if what you heard is what she meant to communicate. Interacting in this way makes your child feel you really respect what she has to say and that it's important to you to understand her point.

Hang in there! Don't overpower your child with your superior mental capacity — focus on listening. It's amazing what can take place when you have a loving attitude and create a safe place for your child to express himself and be heard.

The dictionary is the only place where success comes before work. Hard work is the price we must all pay for success.
– Vince Lombardi, Coach, Green Bay Packers

Clear Signals

Mayor's Wife: "You look nice and cool, Yogi."
Yogi Berra: "You don't look so hot yourself."

Especially with children, the words we say are not as important as how we say them. Trying to disguise things in fancy words doesn't work with kids. They don't buy it. On the other hand, they are forgiving and understanding when you mess up because they sense your good intention behind it.

How we play is crucial to all success. Particularly with children, we need to choose our gestures, body language and tone of voice as carefully as we choose what to say.

Remember that words are just one way of communicating. Our eyes, facial expressions and touch play an important role when expressing our innermost thoughts.

I always understood everything Casey Stengel said, which sometimes worried me.
– Rod Dedeaux, Baseball Coach, USC. As a college coach, Dedeaux earned 10 NCAA championships and sent more than 50 players to the major leagues.

I told him we needed an ultrasound machine and he asked me why we needed music in the locker room.
– Lenny Wilkins, Coach, Supersonics, speaking at a roast for General Manager Zollie Volchok.

To communicate clearly with your child, avoid general statements like, "Clean up your room." Be specific. If you mean "Nothing on the floor," then say so. If you want clothes folded, papers in drawers and books on shelves, let him know that too, so he understands you. Break abstract problems down in concrete, separate things by giving examples. Or even better, show him what you mean by doing it together a few times.

Many children don't have the faintest idea what their parents are making such a fuss about. Organizing, sorting and other abstract concepts are not easily grasped by children. Make your requests specific and be clear about what you expect.

A lack of communication often makes your child look like a loser, when in fact he just doesn't understand what you are talking about. Ask him to tell you what he thinks you mean after you have told him something. You'd be surprised how ineffective communication often is, even when we think we are being crystal clear.

All right, everyone line up alphabetically according to your height.
– Casey Stengal, Manager, N.Y. Mets

Keep It Short!

I stood up and yelled at my wife all week.
– Johnny Kerr, 1966 NBA Coach of the Year, on how he prepared for coaching.

Some parents feel a need to constantly nag and criticize their children in order to "help them grow up!"

"You're hopeless," "Must you always...?" "How many times do I have to tell you not to...!" The only thing these statements do is put down your child and make her feel like a failure. Do you want to have a failure on your team?

If you keep on nagging your child, she is eventually going to give up on trying to get it right and instead sink into hopelessness. At that point, whatever you do or say will fall on deaf ears, and you will have broken your line of communication with your child.

If you feel the need to criticize or correct your child, explain the action you disagree with and why and how it could be corrected. Also add how it affects you. Keep your comments focused on the issue and make it clear it's the action — not your child — you don't like. Make it short, keep it quick, and don't dwell on it.

Leo is a man with an infantile capacity for immediately making a bad thing worse.
– Branch Rickey, General Manager, L.A. Dodgers

Nine Innings in 32 minutes!

The average major league baseball game consists of nine innings and lasts for 2 hours and 45 minutes. In 1910 Mobile played the Atlantic Crackers in the quickest nine-inning game played: 32 minutes. Nobody wasted any time — they swung at everything and ran, to show that baseball is not actually slow game!

After correcting your child for what he has done wrong, quickly move on to expressing your love for him with hugs and words of appreciation for who he is and the good things about him. This is very important: never withhold your love for your child as punishment!

If you set your mind to it, you should be able to correct your child in less than a couple of minutes. After all, a hockey player can make three goals in less than half that time...

Bill Mosienko of the Chicago Blackhawks scored three goals in twenty-one seconds during the final game of the season against the N.Y. Rangers, the fastest scoring spree in the history of ice hockey.

Very well. I just do everything he tells me.

Lee Corso, Football Coach, University of Indiana, explaining how he managed to get along with Basketball Coach Bobby Knight.

Getting Along...

When I was young and smart, I couldn't understand him. Now that I'm older and dumber, he makes sense to me.
– Sandy Koufax, Pitcher, L.A. Dodgers speaking about his difficulty understanding Casey Stengal.

At various stages in your child's development, different communication strategies are required. Communication is the core of every relationship, so we constantly need to keep working at it.

Allow your child to express his or her opinion, and support two-way communication. Keep the focus on a single problem. You can go a long way by taking small steps, one at a time, rather than trying to set a record in the triple jump.

Sometimes being quiet and silently repeating to yourself "I love you," is an amazingly powerful technique that works wonders.

No matter what has been expressed or done, make sure you communicate to your child that he is loved.

I'm very, very speechless.
– Johnny Logan, Shortstop, Milwaukee Braves, on being hired as an announcer.

I want to gain 1,500 or 2,000 yards, whichever comes first.

George Rogers, Running Back, New Orleans Saints, talking about his goals

Goals

If You Don't Have a Target Every Shot Is a Miss

That's the great thing about baseball. You never know what's going on.
– Ralph Kiner, Outfielder, Pittsburgh Pirates

Does that describe your situation or goals for your relationship with your child? If you don't know where you are going, you can't set a course to get you there. The first step on the road to success is to know where you want to go. You wouldn't set out on a trip without having your destination in mind; you wouldn't even know what to pack or which way to head the car. It's the same when hitting the road to a successful relationship with your child.

In other words, you can't get what you want unless you know what it is you want to get.

In order to be a leader, you have to know your job. You have to make people want to follow you, and nobody wants to follow somebody who doesn't know where he's going.
– Joe Namath, Quarterback, N.Y. Jets. Prior to Superbowl III, in which the Jets were to meet the heavily favored Baltimore Colts, Namath "guaranteed" a Jets victory. He knew how to make his teammates follow his lead. In the first AFC win over the established league, the Jets upset the Colts by a score of 16-7.

Getting Your Mind Over the Net

Baseball is ninety percent mental and the other half is physical.
– Yogi Berra, Catcher, N.Y. Yankees

Mental skiing, golf, tennis, and so on, have been developed from the techniques used by star players to prepare themselves mentally to play great and win. If you want to play well and win, don't remind yourself about your mistakes, instead focus on your successes. Visualize yourself as a winner!

It doesn't have to matter how you've seen yourself up to now — from now on see yourself as a winner. To be the most valuable player, you need to start exercising your mind by feeding yourself a positive picture of yourself and your game.

Fantasies! You might snicker. But, even Einstein said that when it comes to imagination vs. logic, imagination will always win.

Be a dreamer. If you don't know how to dream, you're dead.
– Jim Valvano, Basketball Coach, North Carolina State

GOAALL!

Kids naturally do what has been discovered to be a most important tool for success — daydream. How clearly you dream about your success can have a big impact on your level of success. From now on play only successful pictures and tapes in your mind. Remember, we learn by repetition. So keep it up! You have the power to change your track record. You can create a new mental tape of yourself winning the gold, and play it as often as you wish.

> **If you have an objective in life, you shouldn't be afraid to stand up and say it. In the second grade, they asked us what we wanted to be. I said I wanted to be a ballplayer and they laughed. In the eighth grade, they asked the same question, and I said a ballplayer and they laughed a little more. By the eleventh grade, no one was laughing.**
> – Johnny Bench, Catcher, Cincinnati Reds

To Achieve any type of success you need to have a clear and detailed inner picture of yourself, as if you have obtained what you want to win already.

Go for it! Daydream about your success while you are in the shower, car, waiting in line — wherever — and add as much emotion and energy as you possibly can to it. This is a technique many sports players practice daily — seeing themselves perform perfectly in the next game.

> **I'd like to be sort of like Lou Boudreau. He does a good job of recapping the play before it happens.**
> – Johnny Logan, Shortstop, Milwaukee Braves, on becoming the team's announcer

What is your goal? To be the president of your company? Top salesman? A teacher or professor with tenure? Take it from a guy who knows: those are all good and worthy goals, but they won't bring you what you want and need. True success and happiness do not come from material things and dreams coming true. It comes from knowing God. There's nothing wrong with achieving. A person who belongs to God should strive for nothing but excellence. But, set your sight on eternal things, not material.

Joe Gibbs, Coach, Washington Redskins. In 12 seasons as head coach of the Redskins, Gibb's team got to the Super Bowl four times and won three, in 1982, 1987 and 1991.

I believe that if you are bored with life, your problem is that you don't have a lot of goals. You must have goals and dreams if you are ever going to achieve anything in this world.
– Lou Holtz, Football Coach, Notre Dame

If you like winning, you need to keep your eye on the goal in every game in life. To become a champion, keep your eye on your highest goals and let them be your guide, instead of your misgivings.

When you set your goals, keep your eye on winning what is most precious to you in life.

Most areas in life provide only symbols of success and happiness. Having a good job, owning a nice house, wearing expensive jewelry, driving fancy cars — they are all just symbols of success, not the real thing. We are trained to think we need to be successful in order to be loved and respected. But, in your relationship with your child, genuine love is the main ingredient. Loving is what parenthood is all about.

I believe there are certain things that cannot be bought: loyalty, friendship, health, love and the American League pennant.
– Edward Bennet Williams, Owner, Baltimore Orioles

The difference between the impossible and the possible lies in a person's determination.

Tommy Lasorda, Manager, L.A. Dodgers. Lasorda was named National League Manager of the year in 1988, when he coached the underdog Dodgers to upset victories in the National League Championship Series over the N.Y. Mets and in the World Series over the Oakland A's.

Making the Difference...

If you build it, he will come.
– W.P. Kinsella, Author of Shoeless Joe and Field of Dreams

Decide on your goal as a parent and say it in the present tense, as if you have attained it already.

You can't set goals for others: "My kids adore me and love to be with me," is about them, not you. But you can state "I feel very close to my kids and spend at least an hour of quality time with them each day, and I am having a great time!" Or formulate a general goal, like "I'm a great Dad, I laugh a lot and have lots of fun with my kid." Or set a specific one for a problem area such as, "I am successfully assisting my child with her homework, making it fun and easy."

Choose a goal that fills you with enthusiasm and makes you feel passionate. Then write it down on a small card and tape it to your refrigerator, desk, mirror — anywhere you often look — and repeat it aloud several times a day.

I am the greatest!
– Cassius Clay, Jr., better known as Muhammad Ali, Heavyweight Champion of he World. Ali retired in 1980 with a record of 56-4. Others of his openly shared affirmations were "Ain't I beautiful?" and "Float like a butterfly, sting like a bee."

If you have a positive attitude and constantly strive to give your best effort, eventually you will overcome your immediate problems and find you are ready for greater challenges.

Pat Riley, Coach, Miami Heat. At 6'4", Riley was one of the taller players on his University of Kentucky team which — despite being vertically challenged according to basketball standards — still managed to win 27 of 29 games in the 1966-67 season and get to the NCAA championship game.

Challenging Plays

Upsets, Aggressive Plays and Emergency Workouts

I never saw a fucking ball go out of the fucking park so fucking fast in my fucking life.
– Leo Durocher, Manager, N.Y. Giants, on a Willie Mays home run that cleared the left field roof in 1951.

So here you are, a successful Champion Parent with a great attitude, when suddenly your child starts to play a completely different game, pushing all your buttons at once!

Knowing you are your child's number one role model, you think: "But I never did anything like that!" So you start to look suspiciously at your spouse — when you'd be better off taking a look at yourself.

There is a lot to be learned from observing. What is your child trying to do and what is your reaction? Instead of reacting with an old losing strategy like blowing your top, or backing away, try to understand your child's game. Then you will be able to choose a more successful response.

The only gracious way to accept an insult is to ignore it. If you can't ignore it, you try to top it. If you can't do that, you laugh at it. And if you can't laugh at it, it's probably deserved.
– Leonard Patrick "Red" Kelly, Coach, Toronto Maple Leafs

Attention! Attention!

Clowns are not the happiest people in the world. They get into the business because they crave attention. They want people to like them. They want to be loved.

– Max Patkin, Clown Prince of Baseball. Patkin began his entertainment career in front of the crowds at minor league games. During World War II, he played ball in the Hawaiian Army-Navy League. One night, when he was pitching, Joe DiMaggio smashed a fabulous home run. Patkin immediately turned his cap sideways and imitated the Yankee Clipper's trot around the bases.

When your child fights you, perhaps she is just trying to get your attention… and your love.

Everyone carries a deep desire to be loved. With that in mind, you could end almost any fight with one single solution: answer your child's call for loving attention with *Yes, I love you!* But sometimes it's hard for a child to hear those words over the louder cry inside that she is not worthy of being loved. Everyone likes to be reassured and proven wrong in their suspicion that they are unlovable.

Although not always good at relating to his players, Charlie Finley, owner of the Oakland A's during its world championship years of the 1970s, showed he could reach out when, in 1972, Reggie Jackson started the unshaven look that would become an identifying image of the team. Instead of insisting that his players shave, Finley actually offered a bonus to each player who grew a moustache by Father's Day of that season. And when every player took up the challenge, Finley paid off.

Aggressive Plays

Fans don't boo nobodies.
– Reggie Jackson, Outfielder, N.Y. Yankees

To fight for love might seem like a backward approach. But, if we are willing to take a look at the possibility that our child's fights are an attempt to express love — or to get us to express our love for him — we can approach the conflict with compassion and understanding instead of clenched jaws.

If your child starts to fight with you, it means you are important to him. The opposite of love is not hate — it's indifference.

If you are criticized, then you are important.
– Doyt Perry, Football Coach, Bowling Green

Upsets

From 30 paces, "Little Miss Sure Shot," Annie Oakley could hit a playing card on its edge, a dime tossed into the air, or a cigarette in someone's mouth. She could also break six glass balls thrown into the air by firing three double-barreled shotguns at the same time.

It's a shocking experience if suddenly it seems that your wonderful child has turned into "Little Miss Sure Shot," and is aiming at you!

Don't let yourself get caught up in emotions. Screaming at your child or feeling sorry for yourself will not make you a winner. Look at this as an opportunity to practice keeping calm and centered. Instead of getting trapped in your child's game, where you can only lose, let your child become grounded in your calmness. You need to "hold" for your team until the two of you get on with finding your way to the goal, where you will win together.

If you send a team on the field with tears in their eyes, they can't see who to block.
– Bobby Dodd, Football Coach, Georgia Tech

When I'm hitting, the ball comes up to the plate like a basketball. You can see the stitches and the writing on the ball. When you're not hitting, you don't see anything.
– Rod Carew, First Baseman, California Angels

It is interesting how we sometimes fail to see things from our child's point of view. For example, try walking with one arm stretched straight up in the air for a few minutes. It's pretty tiring, yet that's what we expect a small child to do when we hold her hand as we walk down the street with her. Or try sliding down into the seat of your car so you can't see the road, just the sky — that's the way most kids travel, sometimes for hours on end. Or perhaps you've tasted the baby food you feed your child and walked around in a soaking wet diaper.

If your child is upset, try to look at things from her point of view. You might be surprised at what you see.

I slept like a baby – I woke up and cried every two hours.
– Fred Taylor, Basketball Coach, Ohio State University, after a heartbreaking loss

Handling Upsets

You just have to treat death like any other part of life.
– Tom Sneva, Race Car Driver

If your child is upset, communicate your caring and empathy by reaching out to comfort him, and support him in expressing his feelings.

* Create a safe atmosphere for your child. Make him feel that whatever he says is okay.
* Keep your voice low and loving. Listen more than you talk.
* Stay away from loaded questions, and don't make fun of your child.
* Don't stop your child from expressing himself by joking or interrupting him to correct his facts.
* Encourage your child to express not only thoughts, but also his feelings.
* A child might not have words available, but expression in drawing, movement, puppetry, storytelling and fantasy games are other ways of communicating.
* Don't judge the things your child tells you as bad or wrong, or he will not tell you again. Listen and be supportive.

Now I know why they call them Angels. No matter what the pitcher throws, they never hit back.
– Don Riley, Sportswriter, after the 1975 season

> In 1979, the Philadelphia Flyers, in a game against the L.A. Kings, set the record for the most penalty minutes by one team: 188 minutes! The Kings were close behind with 184 minutes! Randy Holt, a defenseman for the Kings, alone tallied 67 penalty minutes – which is especially remarkable considering there are only 60 minutes in a game! But with three major penalties, one minor and five game misconducts, he managed to set his own record.

A certain level of anger and aggression are a natural part of growing up and learning to deal with emotions. Showing your child — through example — how to deal with anger will help him learn to succeed in these areas, too.

By showing your child that your love is always there for him, even when you are upset, you are giving your child a valuable gift of confidence and self-respect. By making yourself bigger than your emotions, you are showing your child a way to win — no matter what.

> One man who didn't have any trouble keeping his balance was John Marino, a teacher from Santa Monica, California, who rode his bike from Santa Monica to New York City in 12 days, 3 hours and 41 minutes. That's 2853.9 miles – and it set a new record!

Emergency Workout Exercises

I like kids when they're kids. I don't like it when they grow up and come to the games and call you names.
– Charles Barkley, Forward, Philadelphia 76ers

If your child seems to be dealing with a lot of aggression and anger at times, it might help to allow for that energy to be expressed. Exercise such as running and punching a bag can burn off that kind of energy. Here are some other ways of working out aggressions and having fun with it!

* Save empty boxes and cartons. Step and jump all over them, or tear them apart.
* Blow up balloons and write things on them. Stick them with a pin, or squeeze them, and see all that angry energy disappear.
* Gather a pile of pillows to punch and scream into.
* Use chalk to draw things that upset you on the garage floor, then step and jump all over the drawings.
* Play loud music – jump, dance and scream!
* Act out pretend games, where you and your child are swimming in calm waters or watching all the upset emotions take off in balloons or clouds passing by.

In the early 1900s, "water baseball" was the game to play. In New York the first game took place in a swimming pool. The hitter had to bat standing in water up to his knees and then quickly swim to first base! This way of playing can really cool you down!

Show me a guy who's afraid to look bad, and I'll show you a guy you can beat every time.
– Lou Brock, Outfielder, St. Louis Cardinals

After your child has expressed her pain, anger or upset, reassure her that it's okay to express all kinds of feelings! Feelings can give us information when we learn to listen to them and express them in a constructive way. Help your child learn to find the message in her feelings, to come up with her own answers, and to develop ways to best handle situations without getting swept up in the feelings.

Help your child get back into the game by cheering her on, and supporting her to refocus on something more fun. If she's a young child, just getting excited about another activity will soon have her on another track. If you have to take something from your child, give her something new to focus on in instead.

If your child is upset because she doesn't want to leave home, a friends house, or wherever, don't just drag her out of there. Create a fun picture of where you are going next. Leaving often causes feelings of loss, but a new focus will ease those feelings.

Baseball is a circus, and as is the case in many a circus, the clowns and the sideshows are frequently more interesting than the big stuff in the main tent.
- W.O. McGeehan, Sportswriter

It's only a game when you win. When you lose, it's hell.

Hank Stram, Coach, Kansas City Chiefs

When You Are Losing

They were booing me at the baggage claim. That's a record.
– Ronnie Seikaly, Center, University of Syracuse, and first round draft choice of the Miami Heat.

It's so bad that the players are giving each other high fives when they hit the rim.
– Ron Humate, Basketball Coach, Southeastern Missouri

We're the only team in history that could lose nine games in a row and then go into a slump.
– Bill Fitch, Coach of several NBA teams, talking about the Cleveland Cavaliers.

We were so bad last year, the cheerleaders stayed home and phoned in their cheers.
– Pat Williams, General Manager, speaking of the Orlando Magic – before Shaq.

All I know is that the way we're hitting, sick people are getting out of bed and wanting to pitch against us.

Bob Lemon, Manager, N.Y. Yankees

Strike One...

I dreamed I'd have a heart attack and die and the obituary would read 'The only NBA coach who never won a game.'
– Don Casey, Coach, L.A. Clippers, on losing his first 19 games

When you feel like you and your child are going through a tough time, look at it as part of the training season — keep a positive focus and maintain your balance. This is a skill that will come in handy in many life situations.

In 19th century Peru the matadors fought bulls on horseback, and the best fighters were women — "capeadoras." The best capeadora, Juana Brena, always fought the bull at full tilt riding sidesaddle, a position difficult to maintain even when one is not chasing a bull. It pays to know how to be successful, even when you're riding off balance.

I am planning to stay positive, even though some negativity is creeping into this team like gangrene in a wound.
– John Salley, Forward, formerly with the NBA champion Detroit Pistons, about the team to which he was traded, the Miami Heat.

The Martial Art of Unfighting

The reason I break bats over the knee is... What I really want to do is tear the whole stadium up, turn it upside down, run everybody out of the stands – just because I didn't get a hit.
– Bo Jackson, Outfielder, Kansas City Royals

If you have a tendency to get worked up and lose your cool when things aren't going well, don't take the risk of letting it out on your child, or anyone else. When you start to feel that you are losing your cool, just stop and take a break, a walk or 10 deep breaths. Don't let your temper get out of control!

Be disciplined enough to stop yourself before you get into a power play with your emotions — because the emotions will almost always win! Put on your sneakers and run around the block a few times. Or buy a punching bag and gloves! This will get you in shape and help you to deal with challenging situations from an intelligent and calm place, instead of doing things you might later regret.

If your stomach disputes you, lie down and pacify it with cool thoughts.
– Leroy "Satchel" Paige, Pitcher, St. Louis Browns

Emotions get in the way of performance.
– Tom Landry, Coach, Dallas Cowboys

Children are extremely sensitive and seem to have a detector that picks up the repressed anger and other emotions of a parent. When the child acts up and gives voice to the parent's repressed feelings, it provides the parent with an excuse to scream and vent some of his anger at the child. So remember if your child acts up, take an honest look in the mirror.

You need to deal with your emotions, for your own sake and your child's. Don't use your child as your vent, but find other ways to release your upset. Handle and sort out your own emotions before you talk, and always discipline your child out of love, not out of anger.

If you scream or use violence against your child in any way, you teach him anger and violence. If you solve your conflicts with words, your child will learn to do the same.

I don't kick lockers or throw bats the way some guys do... There's certainly no real personal satisfaction in an outburst like that. When things go wrong, I try to sit down and analyze what I did wrong and correct it next time. Normally there's an explanation for just about everything.
– Jim Palmer, Pitcher, Baltimore Orioles. In his 19 seasons with the Orioles, Palmer won 20 games or more eight times and had 268 career wins.

Casey could fool you. When he wanted to make sense, he could. But he usually preferred to make you laugh.
– Yogi Berra, Catcher, N.Y. Yankees, about his manager Casey Stengel

---

We have a choice: play our games seriously, with anger and irritation at the slightest upset, or realize that it is all just a game and the goal is to make it fun.

Winning is only half of it. Having fun winning is the other half.
– Bum Phillips, Coach, Houston Oilers

Find Openings And Positive Turning Points!

When I'm on the ice, I look for openings. That's what the game is all about... But when I see something that looks open to me, I go.
– Bobby Orr, Defenseman, Boston Bruins

If you can find an opening that will turn the energy from aggressive or hostile to humorous or loving, you are on your way to becoming a star player.

Sometimes you sense something inside that, when spoken aloud, slams through the emotions and touches the heart. Don't fight it! Give in to the loving, and express it! A smile, that special look, a nod acknowledging that you do understand; inject these into your fight as soon as you possibly can. Look for the smallest excuse or opportunity to hit a home run, or at least get on base!

Sometimes you have to do something extraordinary in the closing moments of a game if you really want to win — like pull your goalie in the last second of an ice hockey game, or throw a Hail Mary pass in football. Look for that extraordinary thing you can do to get the win for your team – there is always something.

In the final analysis, you make your own breaks – in golf as in life. Sure, you'll get some bad ones. But if you can roll with the misfortunes, if you can keep calm and optimistic, you'll get some good breaks, too.
– Arnold Palmer, Golf Pro

Exercise Humor

A manager really gets paid for how much he suffers.
– Gabe Paul, President, Cleveland Indians

Since most of us aren't paid for how much we suffer, suffering and feeling miserable are neither a pleasant nor a successful strategy for winning any game. A positive attitude, humor and playfulness have a much better pay-off — no matter what game you're playing.

Laughter is the best pain reliever. Remember, it's very hard to suffer when you're laughing.

It's up to you whether you are going to suffer through parenthood or make it a fun game to play with your winning team.

They're already talking about changing coaches. They're considering this guy from China. His name is Win Won Soon.
– Pat Williams, General Manager, on the L.A. Clippers losing streak in 1994

A Good Sports Diet

In 1993, when Rookie hockey player Shaun Van Alten, Edmonton Oilers, suffered a concussion in a game and couldn't remember who he was, his coach, Ted Green, is reported to have said, "Good, tell him he's Wayne Gretsky."

All of us prefer to be around people who make us feel good about ourselves and feed us positive messages that we can grow and thrive on. What kind of sports diet are you feeding your child? Do you feed him positive images about himself and your relationship? With your words and actions, who do you tell him he is?

Each evening, make it a habit to comment on what you really appreciated about your child that day, especially after an upset. Make sure you have some physical contact — a hug, a neck rub, a gentle foot massage or high fives — something to stroke away any insecurities left in the child. He needs to be reassured that you still love him, so tell him over and over that you love him and always will, no matter what. *"Thanks for being here and going through things with me, and teaching me how to be a better parent!"*

The more difficult a victory, the greater the happiness in winning.
– Pelé, Soccer Star

Agree to Disagree

In baseball you're supposed to sit on your ass, spit tobacco and nod at stupid things.
– Bill Lee, Pitcher, Boston Red Sox

You don't want your child to be a "yes man," who simply accepts and agrees with everything you say. Independent thinking is not only healthy for your child, it also makes the relationship with him more fun for you, too. Tell your child it's okay to disagree. Some us think if we love someone, we have to agree with them all the time — disagreeing is not dangerous and does not discourage love.

An important lesson to stress to your child is that she can disagree on a subject and still be loved. Discussing crazy topics, rooting for different sports teams, and joking around are great ways to make it safe to disagree. The next time an opportunity comes up, create a positive experience out of disagreement, and it won't create stress or conflict.

We don't care who wins – as long as it's the Cubs.
– Bert Wilson, Announcer, Chicago Cubs

Center Yourself

A baseball game is simply a nervous breakdown divided into nine innings.
– Earl Wilson, Sportswriter

The next time things appear to go bad and you start to lose your temper or perspective, don't panic. Relax, take a few deep breaths and center yourself. Stand up and stretch, look up and take another deep breath. Remind yourself you've got what it takes to turn this into a victory.

The effect on ourselves and others can be dramatic when we take a deep breath and repeat silently, "Peace," or "I love you," as we focus on filling our bodies with calm. In doing this, we not only prevent ourselves from losing control of our emotions, but we also project our calmness to our child, giving him the confidence to step into the safe place we're holding for him.

O.K., now everyone inhale and… dehale.
– Maury Wills, Shortstop, L.A. Dodgers, leading his team through exercise

You can win and still not succeed, still not achieve what you should. And you can lose without really failing at all.

Bobby Knight, Basketball Coach, University of Indiana

Winning and Losing

If a child is provided with the proper environment, he will begin to learn the lessons of athletics which are useful in everyday life – working as a team, self-discipline and personal sacrifice. But if he's thrown against must-win pressures, athletics will become a negative experience and he will soon drop out. If a kid loses, he shouldn't worry about it, but learn from the experience.
– Roger Staubach, Quarterback, Dallas Cowboys

In our eagerness to do the very best for our child, we often think she needs to win every game in life to come out on top. But sometimes the losses and challenges are important teachers — they prepare us for greater success in life.

As a parent, help your children deal with both losses and victories in life in an objective way, and use them as stepping stones to reach the next level of success. Teach your child that winning is not everything — it's just one of many things — and that joy and happiness come from inside, not from winning any game, but from how we feel about ourselves.

It's not whether you win or lose, it's how you play the game.
– Grantland Rice, Sportswriter

It's not how good you are when you play good. It's how good you are when you play bad. And we played pretty good, even though we played bad. Imagine if we played good.

Litterial Green, Guard, Georgia, words spoken after a game when his team beat Georgia Tech by one point

Scoring

Jackie Robinson: "Are you looking for a Negro who is afraid to fight back?"

Branch Rickey: "No. I'm looking for a ballplayer with the guts not to fight back."

When your team is losing, you score by:

* Cooperating instead of confronting.
* Taking control of yourself rather than controlling others.
* Expressing alternatives instead of attacking.
* Understanding rather than getting angry.
* Getting up instead of giving up.
* Reaching out instead of tackling.
* Finding a way to give positive feedback rather than dishing out heavy criticism.
* Setting a good example rather than handing out a penalty.
* Being supportive instead of losing faith.

That is how you score ...

When your team is losing, stick by them. Keep believing.
– Bo Schembechler, Football Coach, University of Michigan

Be a Winner!

Nobody wants to be mediocre in life. The mediocre are the top of the bottom, or the best of the worst, or the bottom of the top, or the worst of the best.
– Lou Holtz, Football Coach, Notre Dame

Be the best no matter what you do in life.
– Walter Alston, Manager, Brooklyn and L.A. Dodgers

It's easy to practice something you're already good at, and that's what most people do. What's tough is to go out and work hard on things that you don't do very well.
– Pete Rose, First Baseman, Cincinnati Reds. For over 30 years, Rose held the record for most career hits. From the beginning of his major league career, Rose was nicknamed "Charlie Hustle."

Do you insist on being the one who comes out as the winner of every argument — always being right or knowing best and never making mistakes? If you make your child a loser, you also lose because you are on the same team.

The term "Blanket Finish" comes from horse racing and refers to the situation where two horses are so close together as they cross the finish line that single blanket could cover both of them. It is much warmer and cozier being close under a blanket with your loved one than alone, high up on a pedestal. Sooner or later you have to come down.

Be sure to make everyone on your team a winner. It might take some work, but it's the only way to play if you really want to win.

Whatever you do, don't do it halfway.
– Bob Beamon, Long Jumper, who set a world record at the 1968 Olympics

Next to religion, baseball has furnished a greater impact on American life than any other institution.

Herbert Hoover, U.S. President

Great Players

How do we teach our children love, loyalty and a longing for excellence? How do we raise great men and women?

All children are born perfect. They are all great beings, here on a very special purpose. The problem is that we, as parents, often fail to see the perfection in each child. We try to mold them into something we think is perfect. We put our own limitations on them in our zealous desire for them to be winners and find happiness.

> **Lombardi would say 'Listen, I know you can't be perfect. But boys, making the effort to be perfect, trying as hard as you can, is what life is all about.'**
> – Bart Starr, Quarterback, Green Bay Packers

No parent looks at his newborn child and says, "How can I screw this one up?" We want to give him the very best, but sometimes we need to remind ourselves that he already has all the beautiful qualities inside of him. Our job is to allow him to bring these qualities out. As champion parents, it's up to us to support our children and remind them how incredible they are.

Spoil your child with your loving, support and caring. Give him time to explore all the different sides of who he is.

Baseball is like church. Many attend, but few understand.

Wes Westrum, Coach, S.F. Giants

Playing the Higher Leagues

I know my days are numbered. I just don't know the number.
– Rudy May, Pitcher, N.Y. Yankees

Our days with our children are numbered. As parents we are often stunned at how fast the childhood years pass, and how we miss the trusting openness, enthusiasm, and unconditional loving of our young children.

Live each day to the fullest, play every game as if it were the last, and treasure each day you get to spend with your children. Embrace every opportunity to do your best to prepare them for life.

Play with your child as if every day was the only day and trust that, if you do your best, everything will come out perfectly in the end.

It doesn't matter who wins or loses, you pray, 'Thy will be done.'
– George Foreman, Heavyweight Champion

I've learned a lot in the past two years. I've learned how precious my wife and children are. I've learned how important it is to serve other people. Most of all, I've learned to put my life in God's hands. The hardest part has been the uncertainty. I had to learn to do what was in my grasp, one day at a time, leaving the rest trustingly to God.

Dave Dravecky, Pitcher, Pittsburgh Pirates, who fought a bout with cancer and returned to pitch again in the majors.

Playing the Inner Field

Some guys play with their head. That's okay. You've got to be smart to be number one in any business. But more important, you've got to play with your heart – with every fiber of your body.
– Vince Lombardi, Football Coach, whose teams won 9 of their 10 playoff games in his 10 seasons as head coach.

Parents who listen to their hearts know how to raise their children in a loving and appropriate way. We already have all the answers we need about how to raise our children — we just need to learn to listen to our hearts more.

A common trait of very successful people is a strong trust in intuition and an understanding of what to do when something "doesn't feel right," or really "clicks."

Listening to your inner self is a way to start strengthening your intuition. It doesn't mean you have to follow everything you hear, but pay attention to small signs from your unconscious, like gut feelings, hunches, images and other conversations from the parts of you that know. Check it out! If it seems to point you in a positive direction, act on it.

My talent is a gift of God — I am only what He made me. You need balance, and speed, and strength. But there is something that God has given me. It's an extra instinct for the game.
– Pelé, considered by many to be the greatest soccer player of all time.

What is the single most important quality in a tennis champion? It comes down to the mental aspect. All champions have that quality. They don't give up, they dig into something extra. People can sense that and see that. That is a necessity if you really want to be considered a champion.

John McEnroe, Tennis Champion, Associated Press Male Athlete of the Year in 1981

Rebounds and Comebacks

The mark of a great player is his ability to come back. The great champions have all come back from defeat.
– Sam Snead, Member of the PGA Hall of Fame, the winningest professional golfer in history.

Keep playing – keep winning. You will take your team even further than you thought you could.

It's not whether you get knocked down, it's whether you get up.
– Vince Lombardi. As a guard at Fordham University he was one of the "Seven Blocks of Granite."

What made me a champion? My father's coaching, training and persistent encouragement paved the way. But it was something more: I was consistent over a long period of time because I never looked back, never dwelled on my defeats. I always looked ahead.

Chris Evert, four-time Associated Press Female Athlete of the year, and a several-time winner of the Grand Slam tournaments.

Forgive and Forget

In 1964, Jim Marshall of the Minnesota Vikings was pretty excited when he got the football following a S.F. 49er fumble. He ran it all the way back to the end zone. A full 61 yards! He made only one mistake — it was the wrong end zone.

Allow yourself and your teammates to make mistakes. And when you do, put them behind you and look ahead. Help your teammate by giving positive decisions for what you are going to do next instead of pointing out all the wrong turns that have been made so far.

The last player to accomplish the fantastic batting average of .400, Ted Williams of the Boston Red Sox, didn't get a hit six out of every 10 times he went to bat. But he didn't become a great hitter by focusing on the misses, nor did he let the misses stop him from continuing to try to hit.

Making mistakes is part of the learning process. Forgiving yourself helps you get rid of guilt and depression. Forgiving others cures resentment, anger and hurt. Both encourage boldness and creativity. Once you forgive, you create free space for other, more successful experiences to come in.

The real champion puts silly errors or unlucky breaks out of his mind and gets on with the game.
– Stan Smith, Tennis Champion

My strongest point is my persistence. I never give up in a match. However I am, I fight until the last ball. My list of matches shows that I have turned a great many so-called irretrievable defeats into victories.

Björn Borg, Tennis Champion, five-time winner at Wimbledon, 1976-1980, known for his ability to retrieve seemingly impossible shots and turn them into winners.

Never Give Up!

You never really lose until you stop trying.
– Mike Ditka, Tight End and later Head Coach of the Chicago Bears

If the game you are playing doesn't work, change your strategy, improve your play or try a new way. But keep playing. The only way you lose with your child is if you stop playing.

It's important to take your team as far as you can — and then be willing to go even further...

I always have good finishes. You go as hard as you can until the end. You can always rest when it's over.
– Janet Evans, Swimmer, the first woman to break the 16-minute barrier for the 1500 meters

A beginner does eight repetitions of a certain exercise with his maximum weight on the barbell. As soon as it hurts he thinks about stopping. I work beyond that point... No human body was ever prepared for this and suddenly it is making itself grow to handle this new challenge, growing through the pain area. The last three or four reps is what makes the muscle grow. This area of pain divides the champion from someone else who is not a champion. That's what most people lack, having the guts to go on and just say they'll go through the pain no matter what happens.

Arnold Schwarzenegger, winner of Mr. Universe and several Mr. Olympia titles

To Change or Not to Change?

Players used to tease Babe Ruth for his habit of putting on the same underwear he used in the game after showering. Babe's answer to this was to simply stop wearing any underwear. However, he didn't let this stop him from modeling a fine line of underwear later in his career.

We can't change anyone but ourselves. Instead, we need to learn to accept others as they are, including our children. Maybe they will never be or do exactly what we would like them to, but who knows — their way may be even better. Each new generation is one step further ahead of the previous one.

You can be the best parent you know how and show your child the most positive path you can imagine for him, but ultimately it's up to your child to choose his own road. You, as a parent, need to accept this and let go. And this might be the hardest lesson of all.

It's what you learn after you know it all counts.

– Earl Weaver, Hall of Fame Manager, Baltimore Orioles

Angels Don't Always Fly High in the Sky

I was trying to will the ball to stay up there and never come down.
– Carlton Fisk, Catcher, Boston Red Sox. Fisk was referring to his winning home run in the twelfth inning of game six of the 1975 World Series. He watched the ball soar from home plate and used vivid body language to will it into fair territory.

Your relationship with your child can't be on a constant high — and you can't be on top all the time. For a ski jumper, staying in the air as long as possible, making the longest jump he can manage, and then landing as elegantly as he can are all part of the game. But so is falling. Repeated falls lead up to those elegant landings.

In your relationship with your child, allow time to practice, fall and fly through the air, too.

Help your children up when they fall and encourage them to try again. And have fun loving them through life, supporting them to make positive choices and to keep trying!

You're the only one who can make a difference. Whatever your dream is, go for it.
– Ervin "Magic" Johnson, Guard, L.A. Lakers

Tomorrow's Saints?

God had a plan for this.
– Reggie White, on the 1997 Super Bowl which was won by his team, the Green Bay Packers.

Il Figlio Di Dio, the famous soccer player, was obviously very popular to earn his name, which in Italian means "Son of God."

You don't know who your child is going to grow up to be: a President, superstar athlete, Nobel Prize winner, perhaps a loving caretaker, an artist, or a creator of peace and harmony in the world. But we do know that all children are special, vulnerable, loving and sensitive. Please treat them gently — nurture and hold them — and then open your hands and allow them to fly...

When soccer star Pele visited Biafra, they stopped the war for three days in his honor.

They're angels in exile... Children are so close to God. They haven't had time to separate from him.
– Muhammad Aitli, "The Greatest Boxer of All Time"

Go out that door to Victory!
Knute Rockne, Football Coach, Notre Dame

Become an Assistant Pocket Coach!

We'd like you to assist us in writing the next Playbook.

If Dad's Playbook inspired you to look for ideas on how to become a Champion Player in all different areas of life, share your success with others. Send us your favorite quotations and a brief statement on how they inspired you to improve your game. If you are the source of a quotation, and we use it, we will credit you in our next book. It's a great way to support each other as parents – and it's fun too!

Dad's Playbook suggests different approaches to becoming a happier parent, but only you know what really works for you and your child! We would love to continue to be a coach on your parent-child team, but we need your feedback and ideas on how we can improve our strategy!

Thank You For Reading!

FeelGoodPress.com

Kids love their parents almost as much as they love ice cream.

This is the only picture we found of all of us wearing clean clothes...

About Åsa Odbäck

Åsa Katarina Odbäck grew up in Sweden, where she graduated #1 in her class from Law School, after which she taught law at the University of Stockholm before proceeding to graduate #1 from Stockholm Business School. She then founded a major success training firm that worked with international companies like Volvo and Ericsson. Later, she served as head of Press and Information for the Swedish Defense University before moving to California where she raised three boys, volunteered as an art and cooking teacher in school, authored five books and started a company to support female artists. While fighting a serious illness, Åsa used art to heal her body and heart, and has since created over 200 paintings. Her most recent shows have been in Los Angeles and Stockholm.

AsaKatarina.com

Designed by Émile Nelson

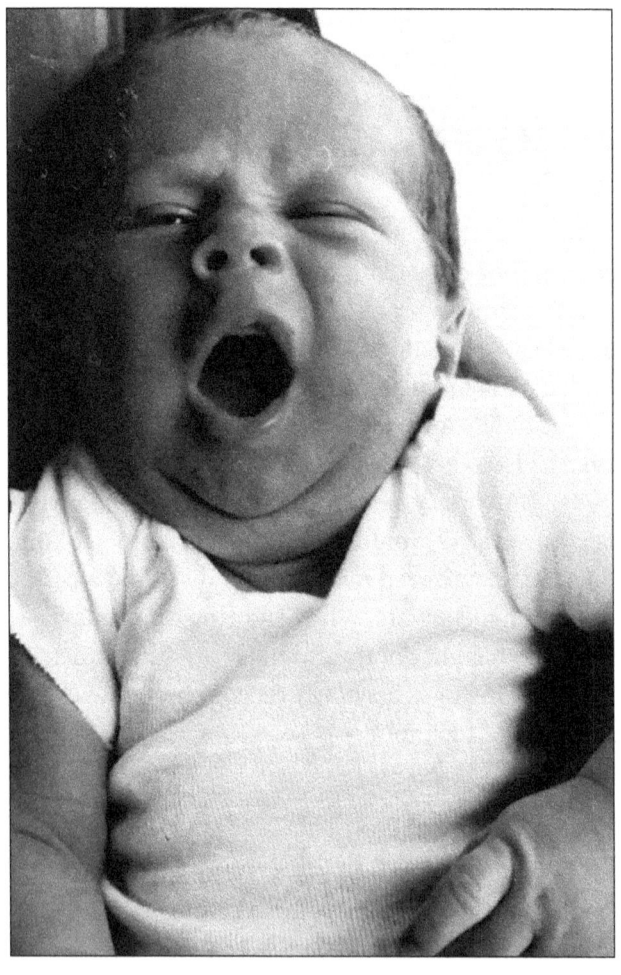

... It really took a lot of energy.

www.ingramcontent.com/pod-product-compliance
Lightning Source LLC
Chambersburg PA
CBHW070554300426
44113CB00011B/1911